DOG TRAINING AND BEHAVIOUR SOLUTIONS:

The Step-By-Step Guide To Solve Common Behaviour Problems.

NADINE EMMERSTORFER

Imprint:

Dog Training
and
Behaviour Solutions:

The step-by-step guide to solve common behaviour Problems.

Cover Design: COLIBRIAN - 99designs
Typesetting and Layout: farhaniqbal786
Image licenses from https://stock.adobe.com

Copyright 2022
Nadine Lichtenegger
Waldstraße 20D
8793 Trofaiach
Austria
nadlichti06@gmx.at

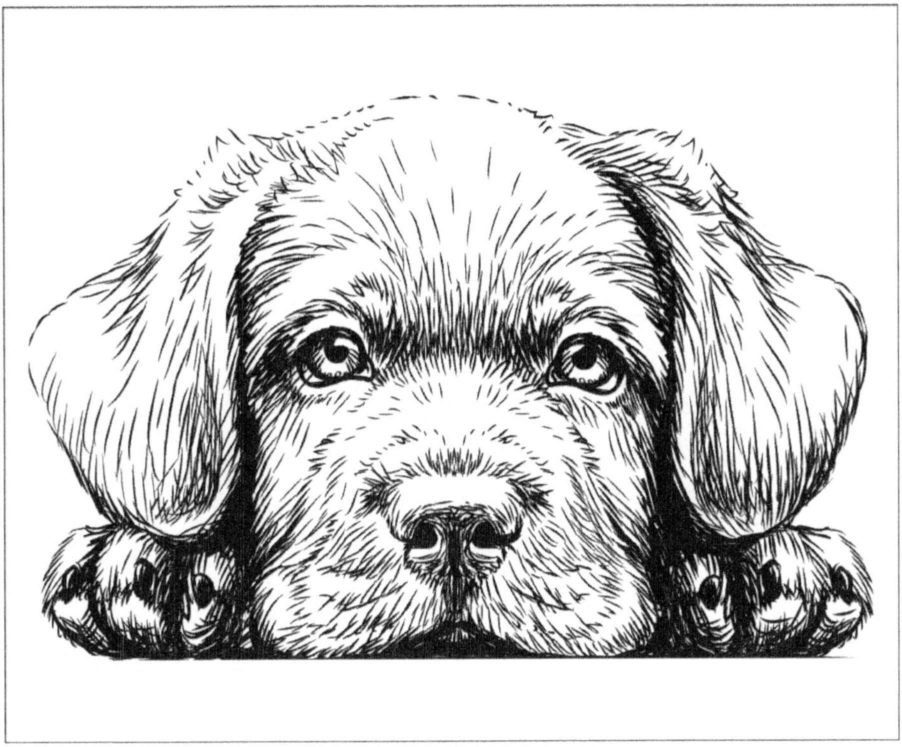

TABLE OF CONTENTS

Foreword	7
Introduction	10
Learn to better understand your dog	13
Impulse control	14
What does this mean?	14
Practical exercises	18
Boosting Frustration Tolerance and How to Strengthen it	22
The bond between human and dog	30
About Feelings	36
Providing Peace and Relaxation	39
General Information	39
Tips for Daily Life	46
Conditioned Relaxation	53
Theoretical foundations for training	60
How do dogs learn?	60

Reward vs. Punishment – what do you have to consider?	74
Rewarding Correctly	77
Applying the Learning Theory Correctly	80

The most common everyday problems with dogs and possible solution strategies — 85

Successful leash training	85
Energetic barking when the doorbell rings	88
The wrong greeting for visitors	90
Problems with feeding	91
Learning to be alone	94
Aggressiveness towards other dogs	96
When your dog chases after cars or bicycles.	99
The dog is missing and the recall doesn't work	100
When hands suddenly become a target	102
The dog doesn't voluntarily give up its bone or toy	105
When the whole garden is dug up	107

Closing words	**111**
Bonus: 92 Dog Exercises	**113**
Source Information:	**114**

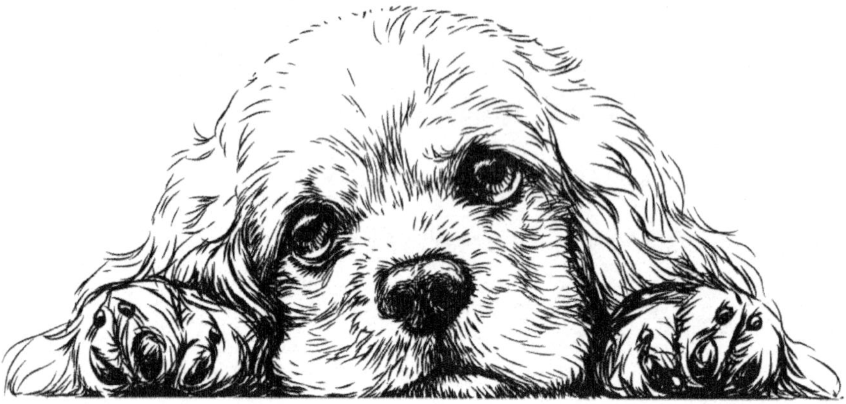

FOREWORD

Surely, you can recall the first excitement when the decision was made that a dog would soon complement your life. The joy was huge and you could hardly wait to finally spend time with your four-legged friend. But it didn't take long for you to be confronted with the first hurdle - education. Unfortunately, this topic is so diverse that there is not one method you can follow that guarantees the success you desire. Research is not easy. If, for example, you were to ask three different dog trainers for advice, you would end up with three different training methods presented at the end of the day. If you want to learn more from the Internet, such as in relevant forums or blogs, or in books, you face a large wall of information that can no longer be overviewed.

The more one reads, the more confused one often becomes. In one place, you hear that you should give your dog as much freedom as possible and only work with treats or other rewards without following a specific system. Other people criticize this approach and advocate for training dogs using only punishment. Additionally, there are countless other opinions that all fall into a gray area. There is no black or white, no right or wrong here. Extreme examples, such as the use of violence, are excluded, of course. Under these circumstances, it doesn't take long to experience signs of overwhelm. You would like to try multiple methods, but this only confuses the dogs even further and they don't know what to do in the end. A stuck situation, which is not easily resolved.

To prevent this and provide you with more clarity, I have written this book.

This is not meant to be another method or collection of training wisdom that is touted as a solution to all your problems, whether it be the regular destruction of your new shoes, aggression towards strangers, or stubbornly ignoring any commands. Instead, we will examine the psyche of your dog and address the root causes of these problems. You will learn to better understand your four-legged friend and use these approaches to find a solution. This will also make training easier, as you will know exactly what you are doing and won't have to blindly follow a method whose background and effects are unclear. Dogs also have emotions and certain behaviors that determine their actions. While each of them has its own character and quirks, aspects such as stress, nervousness, or restlessness do not.

I would like to show you how you can help even the most energetic dog have a confident interaction with its emotions and a balanced demeanor. To do this, we will first deal with the theory, before moving on to practical exercises and common problems.

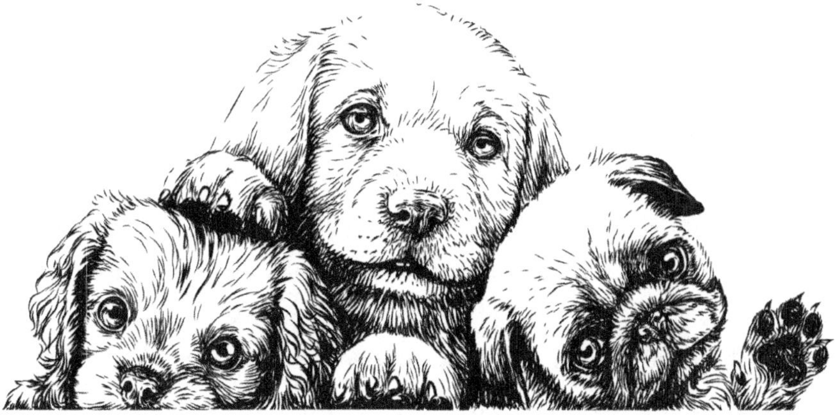

INTRODUCTION

In today's society, we are expected to fulfill various roles and expectations - being a reliable friend, a loving and strong mother, a motivated employee. Dog owners and their pets are not immune to these expectations. It is expected that both parties are as balanced as possible. The dog should be a faithful friend and protector, showing no behavioral problems. He should obey the person's command, enjoy being petted, and only make sounds when necessary. The owner should be relaxed, always in control of their pet, and ensure that their coexistence in society runs smoothly.

If either part of this team strays from the expectations, they will often be laughed at, pitied, or lectured by many people. Gossip quickly spreads, with statements like "Look, he can't control his dog. Is he incapable of training his dog? It's not that hard. And he still can't do it? That's embarrassing. Why did he get a dog?" and so on.

Aside from the fact that most strangers form opinions too quickly when they deviate from their expectations, the pressure on dog owners is often forgotten. Our world is becoming increasingly fast-paced, with so much happening around us that many people face an overload of stimuli every day. The expectations are getting higher, and often one is judged solely on their performance. If everything is not perfect, one immediately faces criticism from others.

What is already difficult for us humans to cope with, affects our four-legged friends just as much. They too will eventually have enough, especially when they realize that their human is constantly stressed. There's no denying that it's not easy to train a dog.

Here's some advice for you: Don't let others stress you out! There will be days when you will question whether all your progress and efforts have been for nothing, and you may feel ashamed. Don't let this lead you to make impulsive decisions, such as letting out your frustration by yelling at your dog. Remain patient and approach the situation with reasoning. Instead of saying "I want my dog to stop these games immediately, pull himself together, and do what I say," you should think "What could be causing this behavior? How does he feel and how can I help him handle it better?" By approaching the situation in this way, you will reach your goal much more easily.

Let others talk all they want, after all, it's not their dog, it's yours. As long as you are in control of the training, you have nothing to fear. I will now show you how to achieve this.

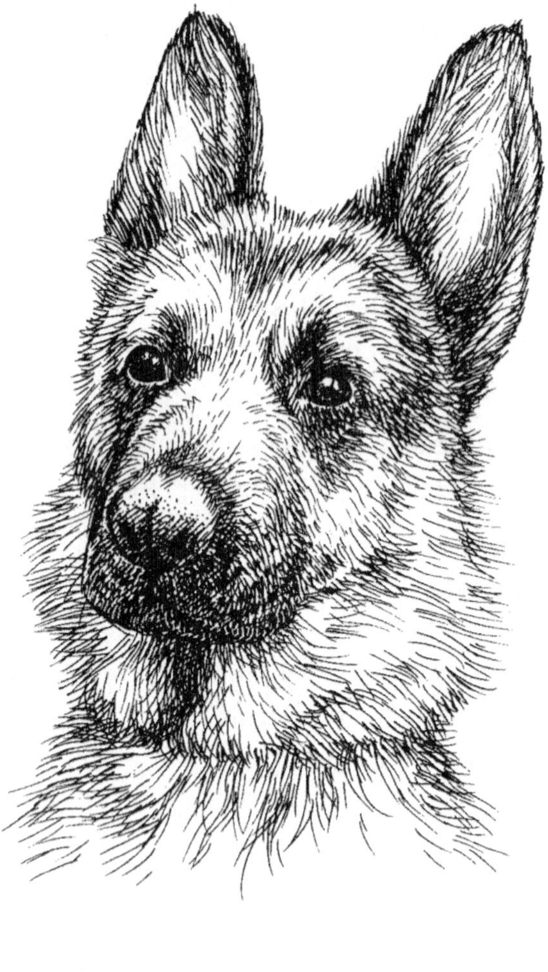

LEARN TO BETTER UNDERSTAND YOUR DOG

In order to get to the bottom of your dog's problematic behavior, it is essential that you understand what causes it. To do this, it's important to always keep one thing in mind: these behaviors do not mean you have made mistakes in terms of education. This concern arises especially when you see other dog owners who seem to have no problems with their four-legged friends - they listen to the word, are friendly to strangers, and get along with other animals. "Why can't it be like this for us?" Many people think in these moments. Be aware that dogs have different character traits. None of them is like the other, which is why dog owners should never compare themselves. What works for others may not have any effect on your dog, which is completely normal. Of course, the same applies in reverse. So don't let others talk you into thinking they have the patent remedy that will turn even the most stubborn nose into the sweetest angel.

You yourself must deal with your dog in detail to find the way to educate him best. Even if this now sounds like a very difficult task, there is no reason to despair. A large factor is the same for every dog:

they act based on instincts and impulses. If you understand, recognize and control these, the rest will be a real breeze. This approach works in any case and makes those methods that call for excessive punishment, constraints and worst of all violence, unnecessary. Even with those four-legged friends who have shown themselves to be highly resistant to education attempts.

Impulse control

Let's move on to impulse control, the most important tool that will accompany you from now on (Impulse control in dogs, 2022).

What does this mean?

The lives of our four-legged friends consist largely of impulses: they are exposed to a specific stimulus and the impulse causes them to react in a certain way. A few examples:

- The dog is presented with food. The impulse is "eat". That means immediately, without any questions asked.
- A rabbit hops around on the adjacent meadow during your walk. The impulse is "interesting, follow", the dog runs off. Whether this happens out of curiosity or from an activated hunting instinct is different.
- A stranger wants to penetrate your dog's territory. The impulse is "defense". He could growl, show his teeth and worst case even bite.

As you may have read, these examples are exactly the kind of behavior that many dog owners want to train their dogs out of and that causes them big problems. That's where impulse control comes in. It can't get rid of the impulses completely, which wouldn't be desirable anyway, but it can help influence them. Let's look at the previous examples:

- The dog is given food. The impulse now reads "Eat yes, but only after my owner has given me the green light." This can prevent him from eating too much, developing food envy or worst of all, eating a poison bait that lies on the road.
- The rabbit hops. The impulse reads "Look yes, but don't chase after it./I am allowed to chase, but only to a certain distance./I am allowed to chase, but must stop and return immediately if my owner calls me." This will prevent your dog from running away and running for miles without listening to you or coming back.
- A stranger comes into his territory. The impulse reads "Defend, but only after seeing how my owner reacts. If the person is a friend or is tolerated, I will do nothing. But if he is an unwanted intruder, then I can defend." This will protect your visitors from being immediately targeted by your dog and being put in danger.

A lack of impulse control is harmful to everyone involved, both for the dog itself and for its entire environment. To simplify the meaning again: impulse control will help him to control his emotions and to steer his actions accordingly. Emotions refer, for example, to those situations in which your dog's character traits are shown. Just think of a hyperactive dog who does not accept a "No" and instead starts to howl out of spite when his human wants to say something – according to the theme "I can't hear you.".

All of this probably sounds like a fairly simple task at first and is well understood, but you need to keep a few things in mind. As I mentioned earlier, impulse control works for every dog – but that does not automatically mean that it always works to the same extent. It can happen that after intensive and consistent training you reach the point where you realize that you simply cannot progress any further. As long as these are only minor quirks and the really problematic behaviors no longer emerge, you need to consider whether you can accept them or support them with other methods, such as conditioning.

The following factors can influence this measurement: the dog's stress level, breed, age, and even body type to some extent. Negative experiences can also play a role. It is observed that larger dogs are less easily disturbed and therefore do not immediately react to all the stimuli they are faced with. This is less the case with smaller and more slender relatives. Furthermore, impulse control makes sense only in most cases with mature dogs, as the corresponding brain areas are not fully developed in younger dogs and they are subject to childish curiosity that is difficult to control. This does not mean, however, that you cannot still approach the exercises. This way, the dog gets used to it from an early age and you can really get started when it reaches the appropriate age. As far as the breed is concerned, you should not underestimate this influence either: it is much easier to untrain an unintended pursuit of a fleeing wild animal in a watch dog, such as a Rottweiler, than in a typical hunting dog, such as a German shorthair. Each breed has its typical characteristics and therefore reacts very differently to different impulses.

Furthermore, you should also control yourself a little in terms of the training volume. The impulse control exercises are very demanding for dogs, as they run counter to their natural instincts and they can only with difficulty adapt to them. Therefore, they should not be repeated too often in succession and aim for lighter, but longer training, to ensure success and not overload the animal.

Regarding achievements: Wisely choose the environment or the subject of your training. Everyday life with a dog can often be stressful and there are often problematic situations that you would like to make disappear. Whether it's the repeated refusal to lie down in the designated sleeping place or the aggressive attack on the postman. Definitely differentiate here! Determine what is of top priority for you and in which situations it is especially important that the dog can reliably control his impulses. Train these first to ensure the safety of everyone. Only then, when there is nothing to fear in this regard, can you focus on the less important aspects. If they still pose a problem, if you can deny them and handle them well, then you should spare your four-legged friend the additional effort.

The last thing to consider: Even if you jokingly compare the education of dogs and children, never forget that dogs do not have the same cognitive abilities. If you teach your child to always treat other beings with respect, it will apply this lesson in all possible situations: with a fragile butterfly, a large horse, or the strenuous classmate from his class. However, it is not possible for a dog to automatically transfer what it has learned to another situation. If you train him to stop chasing after a fleeing cat, it does not mean that he will never chase after a cyclist again. You start from scratch with each new problematic situation. So it can be said that you need perseverance and consistency when you start impulse training.

Do not let this discourage you, because once you have the hang of it, it is only a matter of time before the desired results are shown. Support your dog actively with praise and treats during this time so that he realizes that he benefits from his impulse control and can better engage. Other activities that he enjoys very much, such as playing together, cuddling, a trip to the dog park, bathing, are also optimal training endings. Avoid punishments as much as possible to avoid causing additional stress. This also prevents success.

Practical exercises

Now I would like to introduce you to some exercises that aim at impulse control.

1. **Seeking Eye Contact** (Nubi, 2022): This exercise is about communicating to your dog that they should look at you first before moving on. This can be useful in various situations as a foundational skill. For example, they can only eat if they first look at you and you give the "Okay," or they can only leave the "Stay" and start running after they first look at you.

   How to Practice:

   First, take a treat in each hand.

   Now your dog should be waiting in front of you. "Sit" is a good option, "Down" and "Stand" are also fine.

   Extend your hands. Your dog will already have detected that you have treats and their full attention will now be automatically directed towards you. It may be that they first think for a few seconds and focus on your hands. Give them time. Sooner or later, they will look directly at you, as they expect another command. Only when they do this and consciously maintain eye contact, will they be rewarded with food.

2. **Waiting for Treats** (Impulse Control in Dogs - Free Exercises, 2022): The goal of this exercise is to train the dog not to immediately snap at the treat, but to patiently wait for release.

How to practice:

Take another treat in your hand. Close your hand and squat in front of the dog, with your hand relaxed in front of your body. Squatting is actually one of the most important aspects here, as it puts you at the same level as the dog and makes the food theoretically reachable for him, since you're not holding it a foot above his head this time.

Many dogs will already show some reactions. Some will try to move you with their paws to open your hand. Others will carefully lick or nibble on your fist. Sometimes you can observe them performing a whole repertoire of learned tricks and stunts, since they have been rewarded with food in the past. Whenever your dog shows such behavior, respond with the word "No". Besides that, don't do anything. It's now up to your dog to figure out what this word means. The only thing required of him is to simply pause for a few moments and wait. What is important here: especially in the beginning of training, the dog will not yet show the desired patience. Recognize the moment when you see the first promising signs: he remains sitting or standing quietly, looks at you or away, and refrains from the unwanted behavior. Reward him now with the treat, accompanied by a rewarding word such as "Fine" or "Good".

This exercise can be further increased if the dog becomes noticeably calmer and waits instead of getting nervous because he doesn't know what to do. You can then make him wait a little longer and include eye contact. If that works smoothly, you can also challenge him by opening your hand and presenting him with the food. At this point, you can nicely see how your dog's impulse control is: either he will continue to look at you and patiently wait for you to give the green light, or he will not be able to resist temptation and try to eat the treat directly from your hand. If that happens, silently close your hand and return to the previous procedure.

3. **Maintaining Position** (Nubi, 2022): Your dog should learn to maintain positions such as "Sit/Down/Stand", even when he is distracted. This is particularly important when you are out in nature together and encounter other animals such as rabbits or deer that your dog would love to chase after.

    How to Practice:

    First, let your dog take up the desired position. For this exercise, your dog should already be familiar with and know how to hold these positions for a few seconds or until the next command.

    Now a second person enters the picture, who will be your training partner. Together, create some distractions: If the person has a dog, they can walk by with their dog during the exercise. This works particularly well if the dogs either get along very well or can't stand each other. There are many other possibilities: The person could walk by alone, ride by on a bicycle, call the dog, present a treat, wave their favorite toy around, or throw a ball. If your dog manages to maintain the position and not give in to his impulse, reward him. Make sure the reward is appropriate! If your dog loves to eat, he should get his favorite treats. However, if a toy is more important to him, use that instead. Reward him by throwing a ball yourself, playing tug of war, or similar activities. The dog should realize that the reward is just as good as the impulse that he misses during this exercise, otherwise he will quickly lose interest.

4. **Expecting the release command** (Nubi, 2022): This exercise is similar to the previous one, but the temptation is a bit greater. Accordingly, it is suitable if the dog already has some training experience.

    So it is practiced:

    Have your dog take a desired position. Then move away from him. At first, a few steps are enough, with enough experience you can even go out of sight. Now it's time to introduce a targeted stimulus. Here you can let your creativity run wild: Maybe his favorite playmate "accidentally" walks by, maybe a ball flies over his head or a frisbee is thrown if he likes to play catch. If the dog is still in his starting position and was able to successfully resist, go back to him relaxed. Reward him in this position. This is very important, only then can the dog associate the reward with maintaining this posture. Then signal to him through a previously learned release command, such as "Go" or "Now," that he may now follow the stimulus and play.

5. **Change direction** (Sporrer, 2022): This exercise is about placing a temptation in clear view, then running in the opposite direction. This helps your dog learn to expect and handle the

possibility of having to resist the temptation, even if you want him to.

Here's how to practice:

During a small walk, your dog should have a solid "heel" command. First, use a command like "Stay" to hold your dog in place, then throw a treat or toy. The throw should be clearly visible so your dog knows exactly where the object of desire is waiting for him. Then, turn around and go in the opposite direction, gradually getting farther away. If your dog calmly walks next to you without trying to pull you towards the object, you can reward him by letting him go and get it. Later, you can make the exercise more challenging by running in the direction of the temptation instead. This will teach your dog to wait for your command even though it's right in front of his nose.

Boosting Frustration Tolerance and How to Strengthen it

Another important issue that goes hand in hand with impulse control is frustration tolerance (Frustration Tolerance in Dogs - Exercises to Try, 2022). A dog must learn to tolerate a certain level of frustration without immediately taking action, such as pushing, making noises, becoming nervous, or even aggressive. After all, you don't always have the time or desire to immediately respond to every small need and leave everything else standing or lying.

To further highlight why frustration tolerance is particularly important in relation to impulse control training:

- An impulse triggers a certain reaction or desire in the dog. For example, he may want to catch a ball that flies over him or immediately start eating when his favorite food is placed in front of him.
- If, for example, this impulse is suppressed through your training or you don't respond to it, negative emotions are triggered in the dog. At the beginning of the training, this can happen quickly - your four-legged friend is not used to the previous status quo no longer existing and a lot will change. If he used to feast to his heart's content without having to wait, he will be confused when the opposite is now the case. The result: frustration builds up.
- This is where frustration tolerance comes in. It allows your dog to endure frustration better and longer or even prevents it from happening so quickly.

Not only will it make training easier, but it will also improve your daily life together. In addition, you can enjoy the following benefits:

> Your dog can stay home alone for longer periods of time without worrying about boredom or stress causing damage to your home.

> He will show less unwanted or uncontrolled hunting behavior. Hunting dogs with special training are excluded, as this is shaped under separate circumstances.

> Your dog will become more independent and can entertain himself. He will no longer feel the compelling need to follow you everywhere and always be with you to feel like he belongs.

He can better relax in daily life and will not get nervous so easily if you want to enjoy a quiet afternoon without constantly doing something.

On your walks, he will be easier to keep "at heel" and will not pull on the leash as strongly, as he will not be so easily distracted by training. He will explore his surroundings more calmly and patiently.

Your dog will be quieter in terms of his sounds. Strongly frustrated dogs tend to bark, whimper, or howl when they want to assert their will or convince their owner to take a certain action. This will no longer be the case with you.

Do you know if your dog is frustrated and if some of its behaviors are influenced or caused by this? Of course, every dog experiences and displays frustration in different ways. However, it can still be easily recognized. Most of the affected animals are very restless and loudly give signs that they are dissatisfied. Stress panting can also be a sign. Whenever there is no other plausible reason for panting, you can assume this. Other signs would be low tolerance for boredom: The dog can't stay alone well and you have to worry that shoes or furniture have suffered when you come home. Perhaps he's digging one hole after another in your lovingly maintained garden. When walking, there may be pushing, pulling, or even biting the leash when important incentives are missing. Most dog owners would agree here and claim that this is the behavior they absolutely want to avoid.

However, a serious mistake often happens: Some people give in so that their dog will stop. They give in to their dog's will and perhaps don't think much of it, after all, they don't want to embarrass themselves in front of others, just want peace and quiet, or are already so stressed that they can't take any more and look for the easiest way out of the situation. And once won't be that bad, right? Unfortunately, it actually is. On the one hand, our four-legged friends are anything but dumb and will remember that under circumstance XY, they were able to assert their will through certain behaviors like pulling or barking. This means they will try this more often in the future and it will become increasingly difficult to untrain them. On the other hand, it can happen that we humans quickly become neglectful. If you have once crossed that line, it may be that you will act this way more often in the future. It wasn't that bad at the time, you finally had peace and were satisfied, just like the dog was. A short-term illusion of harmony, which we actually so much desire. Some give in to experience this longer. Others don't think further and act unintentionally. The result is always the same. Always be aware that giving in is not a solution when it comes to frustration tolerance! You need as much perseverance in training as your dog does. You must be able to endure it when your dearest companion looks at you with his most charming Dachshund gaze and just wants a little food. Similarly, you must endure that he barks continuously and just won't calm down, even if you are completely exhausted and already crawling on your gums.

Although it may be demanding and a lengthy process, frustration tolerance can be trained effectively. Here I would like to introduce some exercises that you can apply. Keep in mind that not every exercise will be suitable for you or your dog. Just as the different expressions of his impulses, the circumstances that trigger frustration are highly individual. For some, it is mainly being alone, for others it is waiting for food. Observe your dog closely and find out how he reacts to different things. Adjust the exercises accordingly to achieve the greatest success.

1. **Suppress Control Behavior** (Frustration Tolerance in Dogs - Exercises to Do, 2022): This exercise aims to help your dog

stop following you everywhere. If they always accompany you like a shadow inside your own home and you can't even find peace on the toilet, something needs to be done. It may seem at first like your dog can't be without you for a second, but in most cases, this is actually control behavior. It appears to them that they cannot leave you alone. This creates stress for everyone involved and makes it difficult for the dog to relax at home.

Here's how to practice:

Initially, your dog will be encouraged to stay in one room or in a specific area. For starters, you can leash them. This may feel strange inside your home, but it is not harmful and serves its purpose effectively. Now, walk around your home for a while. First cross the room, then go a little further away and out of sight. Ignore your dog's reactions and continue this until they lie down quietly and relax on their own. Once this happens, you can un-leash them. In this way, they will learn that nothing bad happens when you move around your home without them. It is very important to not use any commands during the entire exercise! You should not compare this environment with the "outside world" where it is essential for them to listen to commands. At home, these commands, except in exceptional cases, are not necessary. The goal should be that you can move freely without giving commands or anything similar.

2. **Waiting to Play** (Frustration Tolerance in Dogs - Exercises to Follow, 2022): The following situation is familiar to many people, especially with young and energetic dogs: when they

see their favorite playmate, they either pull with all their strength on the leash or immediately sprint off, with their ears set to full speed. What the human says is simply ignored because immediate play has absolute priority. This also needs to be stopped. Of course, every dog should be able to play as they please, but only when you allow it and after they have calmed down a bit.

So it is practiced:

To maintain control in these exciting situations, make sure to keep your dog on the leash. Now meet the other person with the playmate, who should also be leashed for this exercise. Stand a little distance apart from each other so that the dogs can't touch each other. Keep the leashes short or make yourself ready, the main thing is that the four-legged animals are fixed. Now first talk calmly, maybe there are exciting news you want to tell each other before playing. It is likely that it won't take long before the dogs start pushing. Both of you should ignore them. Let all reactions go over you until both dogs have completely calmed down. Only then can you leash them. To continue the exercise: Do not allow your furry friend to immediately run off after leashing. Have them sit with "Stay" first and then release them after a moment. Then they can play to their heart's content.

3. **Resisting Treats** (Quast, 2021): This is about the dog being able to resist food, even when it's served to them on a silver platter. They should learn that there's only something if it's either feeding time or they've earned it explicitly.

How to practice:

First, have your dog quietly lie down within your home. Now take a few treats and throw them in front of him into the room. To start, aim for as great a distance as possible – so that he can clearly perceive the food, but still think "That's so far away, I'll just pretend it's not there." This way, he won't be tempted so quickly and can resist better. If he now remains relaxed, praise him and reduce the distance to the food the next time. If he wants to get to the food at a certain point, remove it and go back to a greater distance to make it easier for him. The goal should be that he doesn't start eating immediately, even if a treat is right in front of his nose and he just needs to open his mouth.

4. **The Relaxation Exercise** (Quast, 2021): Some dogs want their owners to give them attention whenever they want it, which can take up a lot of the available leisure time. This exercise is meant to teach the dog that it can relax even when there is nothing to do or when the owner doesn't have time or desire to give attention.

    How to practice:

    There are several variations of this exercise. You can either do it while you're out in nature/city or at home. The core remains the same: Whenever your dog insists on attention and expresses this loudly, ignore it until it stops this behavior. Do not try to calm it down. Even just saying "Shh" or "No" gives it the desired attention and thereby its way. Once it has stopped and relaxed, you can end the exercise. If you were just walking with it and talking or taking a break on a bench, you can continue walking. If you were at home, you can reward it with a "Good boy/girl". Please refrain from using treats - the dog should learn to calm down of its own accord and that a little boredom is not a bad thing, rather than only exhibiting this behavior because it expects food."

5. **Resisting the Toy** (Quast, 2021): Similar to food, the dog should learn not to grab the toy immediately when it is within reach.

    How to practice:

    A training partner is needed for this exercise. It would be ideal if the partner's dog is one of your dog's favorite playmates and there is a specific toy that both love to play with. Your dog should stay on the leash and take a seat next to you. The playmate should start playing with the toy. Your dog must first watch quietly. If he remains relaxed and waits for your release, praise him. You can also use treats here. As with the other exercise, you are working over distance. If your dog can resist, the training partner will come closer in each subsequent training run until eventually your dog is no longer bothered when playing with his favorite ball right in front of his nose. Even if you later reward him with words or food, don't forget to play with him extensively afterwards.

In addition to increasing your dog's frustration tolerance, it also boosts its resilience. This is similar to how humans grow from challenges and become stronger after overcoming a problem. We learn to adapt to new circumstances and develop better strategies for future situations. Although dogs lead a much simpler life and don't face as many challenges as we do, psychological stress or negative emotions should not be underestimated in them. As your dog increasingly learns to tolerate these negative emotions for longer periods of time, to better process them, or not to build them up, its inner self will be strengthened. It will become more emotionally stable and better equipped to handle future problems and even find solutions on its own.

The bond between human and dog

Every dog owner knows this special feeling when he thinks about his dog: he is much more than "just a pet", as some people would say. He is a loyal companion, full-fledged family member and one of the best friends you can have. For some, this status goes beyond and the quadruped becomes something like a substitute child. There is disagreement about how far one should go in this regard. One feels comfortable when the beloved dog lies next to him during dinner and enjoys his finest premium steak, while the people only have scrambled eggs today. Others keep their dog in his pen for half the day and only spend time with him when they feel like it. There are countless other ways to lead a life with a dog. However, every owner asks himself one question: How does my dog feel about me?

After all, you love him more than anything, but sometimes you're in the dark when it comes to how it looks the other way around and what he thinks about his master. Nevertheless, you shouldn't just accept that and instead focus on the bond with him. This can change a lot in your interaction, both positively and negatively. If you want to understand your dog completely and help him, this is one of the points to consider.

Let's move on to general information regarding bonding (Doguniversity [Doguniversity - Dog Training with Daniel], 2020):

When you see a dog-owner pair relaxing comfortably on a park bench, you're happy for them. The person is sitting on the bench, reading a book, and relaxing, while the dog is lying down and dozing off in front of him. He has his head and front paws on his owner's shoes, as if snuggling up to him. For many, this is the optimal state, as far as you can tell from this brief moment. If you asked several people about it, the vast majority would likely confirm that these two definitely have a strong bond with each other. However, it's not that simple. There's often confusion between the actual bond and the relationship.

Relationship vs. Bond:

So, one must first become aware of the difference between these two terms. The relationship refers to the component that is easily recognizable to outsiders. You only need to observe how the human and dog behave in the presence of each other: Do they look at each other, without reason, into each other's eyes? Do they seek each other's proximity and enjoy it? Is the dog respectful towards its owner and listens to what he has to say? If you can answer these questions with "yes," these are indicators of a good relationship with each other. But that does not mean much, because the relationship itself says relatively little. This is simply because social beings have a relationship with everyone who comes into contact with them, no matter how fleeting. You have a relationship with the intern who completed his two-week practical part in your department five years ago, just as you have a relationship with your best friend. Dogs are no different.

Bonding refers to a strong emotional component that only occurs when one cultivates a positive relationship with the other. Both parties feel comfortable with each other and there is a strong trust that prompts both to let go and fully relax with one another. The latter point will become increasingly important. It is also true that bonding partners are a great social support for the dog. When such a partner is present, the quadruped feels safer, becomes braver, and can therefore more easily cope with difficult situations than if it had to handle them alone. Stress is also reduced and dealing with negative emotions becomes easier. This can be seen especially well when someone has two or more dogs, among which two have a close bond with each other. When they are together, they act as if they've been exchanged and exhibit a behavior that makes one believe that the two could conquer the world together. However, if they are separated, nothing is left of this. They would not behave this way with any other dog. Bonding partners are not interchangeable.

Imagine this: you have had the dream of taking a three-month vacation in Australia since childhood. You have been happily in a relationship for ten years and could easily imagine fulfilling this dream together. Could you also imagine going with your co-worker, who you have known for a long time and consider to have a bond with? You can have great conversations with this person, share almost everything, and trust each other. Would you still take this step with them and replace your partner without batting an eye? Most likely not. It's the same with dogs. They can have multiple bonding partners, but each bond is different and special and can't be achieved with anyone else.

How can you recognize the bond?

Now the following question arises: If I can't see and assess the bond, how can I recognize how my dog feels about me?

It is not easy for you alone, but there are some indications. A big indicator would be "contact lying," in which the dog comes to you, seeks your proximity and stays with you without you having to motivate him. Moreover, it is not so easy, because the dog's attachment system is not permanently active - in most cases it only shows when its attachment partner is no longer with him. A dog trainer would test this by exposing the dog to a special training scenario. For example, he would have the owner leave and observe how the dog behaves. Alternatively, threatening situations are used in which a dummy "attacks" the owner or similar. Does the dog defend his owner or does he have fear and run away, leaving him to his fate? Based on these reactions, the professional can assess how the attachment of the two stands.

But not every dog owner has the time, money, or desire to go to a dog trainer. You can stage such a separation situation yourself by spending time with your dog at home and then leaving the room without taking him with you. Before you do, place a camera so that you can record exactly how he behaves. If your dog would simply follow you, you can close the door behind you and force him to experience this new state and the emotions it triggers.

It can be simpler: Observe his behavior when you go for a walk together. Provided you are in a relatively low-stimulation environment and you have not given him a command like "heel" - where does he run? Is he by your side for the majority of the time and makes contact by touching you occasionally? Or does he simply leave you alone, choose his own pace and occupy himself with everything else? The result says a lot, so pay close attention the next time.

How close should the bond be?:

The closer the bond, the better - right? Wrong. A bond that is too close is anything but nice and greatly affects the quality of life of the partner who is more bonded. It would mean that he is completely dependent on him and would never like to leave his side. Whenever his bonding partner is not with him, he experiences stress and sadness, cannot be alone well. He has nothing else to do but lie around aimlessly and wait until the other comes back. In the meantime, there's nothing that would bring him joy. The partner would be the only source from which he draws happiness and joy in life. That's not good for either the human or the dog. So: the bond should only be close enough that both enjoy each other's presence and enjoy it, but not dependent on it. They should be able to enjoy life alone, but if the bonding partner is there, it's just a bit nicer.

Even though it's nice to be special in your dog's eyes, it's important to make sure that your dog has multiple attachment figures. These can be other people or other animals. This is especially useful when you can't spend time with your furry friend, for example if you want to travel for a longer period of time and can't bring your pet with you, or if you have a prolonged hospital stay. In these cases, your dog will have another attachment figure who can comfort them and get through the time until you return without suffering. These attachment figures can't be conjured out of thin air or forced. Don't put too much pressure on yourself and let yourself be surprised by the social connections your dog will make.

How can one work on the bond?:

Every owner wants to have a strong and healthy bond with their dog. If this is checked and it turns out that this is not the case, disappointment is great. One wonders if this is something personal and if one could not change anything about it. I can reassure you that it can be changed. The bond cannot be forced, but there are a few things you can do. Basically, improve and strengthen the relationship with each other, only then will the bond arise. Have fun together and do a lot together. Give him attention and show that you are interested in him and want to understand him. Set boundaries, but respect his as well. Give him protection, encourage him to be braver and to step out of his comfort zone because you are keeping his back free. Overcome difficult situations together. Give him clear guidelines. And most importantly, be patient and confident, approach everything without expectations. You don't have to prove anything to your dog or win his favor, just as you shouldn't be trying to please people you want to like you. Authenticity and a strong character are key here.

Can you make mistakes in this regard?:

"Yes, unfortunately. However, only if you adopt a false expectation and do not have the necessary patience. Some people believe they can speed up the bonding process by using pointless rewards such as treats or buying a lot of toys. They want to express how much their dog means to them and are happy when the dog reacts positively. This initially appears to be strengthening the bond. This is true, but on a false basis. These dogs are then materially bound, but not socially. They realize that they only need to give their owners a little bit of attention to get something in return. If this material component is removed and nothing is bought or cooked extra for the dog, the true face of the bond is quickly revealed: in most cases, the dog will turn away because its owner is completely unimportant to it. You cannot buy a bond, only create it."

What else should be taken into consideration?:

Let's return to the initial example of a dog and its owner on a park bench: At first glance, this situation appears to be really great, however, there is a small indication that something is not right: the dog has partially rested on its owner's feet. Such behavior often has nothing to do with positive contact lying and instead has more to do with the dog's unhealthy control behavior. Other indications would include "stalking," constantly following even to the bathroom, lingering in doorways, and positioning in front of the owner. Of course, the dog can walk in front of you while on a walk, but if it never leaves this position and never walks beside or behind you, this does not demonstrate a strong and respectful bond. Also, if it puts one paw or even more on your feet, it wants to control you a little bit. If you notice such behavior, it is extremely important to intervene immediately.

About Feelings

We have now established that dogs also experience emotions and perceive them in humans. When one is very sad and crying, the best friend is often by our side within a few moments, snuggling up and cheering us up. If one is very happy and excited to see him, he reacts to it and is infected by it (Colino, 2021).

There are several studies (A shoulder to cry on: Heart rate variability and empathetic behavioral responses to crying and laughing in dogs, o. D.), which prove that dogs not only recognize how their owners feel, but are also infected by the same emotions. This is due to the fact that our dogs often rely on us when assessing a situation. When we meet strangers who they don't know, everything is still open: is this person a threat or a long-time friend? They don't know how to behave, so they pay close attention to how we do. If we humans now radiate calm, are relaxed and happy, this means for the dog that the situation is safe and there is no cause for concern. As a result, he will relax. The same applies to stress, fear and other negative emotions. They show empathy, because in people they feel particularly connected to, they are able to perceive their emotions purely through instincts.

It's similar with humans. For example, consider if someone smiles at you for no reason - this triggers positive feelings in you and you are prompted to smile back. Dogs and humans have similar instincts in this regard, which can trigger a true ping-pong game of emotions. The gestures and facial expressions of dogs can be compared to ours and therefore relatively easily interpreted. This can result in us seeing that our dog is tense and stressed, which in turn puts us under pressure. All this happens subconsciously. It may be that the dog is reacting this way only because we did it first and he is just copying us. So it goes back and forth and both carry a disadvantage, even though it is not clear who started it and why.

But not only that, dogs also interpret the sounds we make and changes in our natural scent. In a way, we're like an open book to our dogs and it's not easy to hide anything from them. This can have its disadvantages, but it speaks to the very close relationship between humans and dogs that can't be observed between any other two species. Moreover, sharing emotions together bonds them even more, so don't be afraid that your dog will see through you and make you more vulnerable. You can see him as a kind of mirror. Whenever your dog is stressed, scared, or angry, ask yourself: Are you maybe experiencing the same thing without admitting it? By reflecting on your own feelings, you'll do yourself a favor, which will save you and your four-legged friend a day or two.

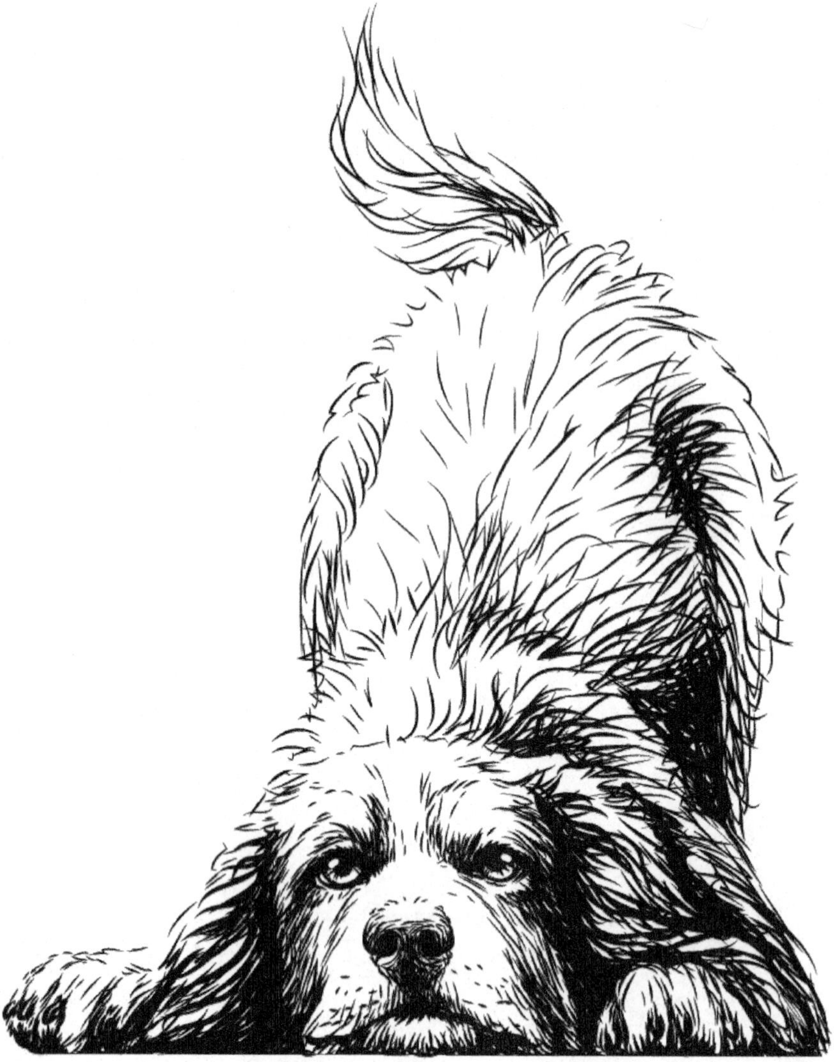

PROVIDING PEACE AND RELAXATION

A good training is half the rent and will help even the most energetic four-legged friends to calm down. This does not mean that you can't intervene in a supportive way. Every dog needs a lot of peace and relaxation, which is often underestimated. That's why I would like to list some additional information for you in this chapter (Causes & Reasons for a Restless or Stressed Dog [Part 3], 2022).

General Information

Firstly, it can be said that dogs need more downtime than many think - up to eighteen hours a day. When you read a number like that, you probably think first of cozy cats who spend most of the day lying or sleeping. Does this claim apply to a dog who stands in front of you several times a day with a wagging tail, waiting for it to start? This is actually the case. We must not forget that dogs are not machines that can be in action around the clock and only fall when they run out of strength. They would participate to a certain extent, but this is counterproductive.

Remember the number of stimuli we are confronted with on a daily basis, especially in cities. It's loud, there's always something to see, and there are many different smells to experience. Imagine this from the perspective of a dog who experiences all of these impressions much more intensely than you do—and in a world that they can only understand to a fraction. Their heads are constantly flooded with stimuli and their brains are working at full speed to process all the impressions. So give them the opportunity to relax and not be unnecessarily overwhelmed by providing them with additional peace and quiet. Even if it doesn't always seem like it, there are many things happening in their heads that are more than just "eat-play-sleep." Slow down their daily life and give them the opportunity for reflection. You might also want to use these quiet breaks for yourself, as they are also very convenient for us humans.

In summary: Exercise does not equal overexertion. A dog does not need to be completely exhausted to be happy, listen better or for what may be assumed. Of course, breed-specific exercise is important, but it is also important to provide regular breaks. The problem is, if your dog does not get enough rest and sleep, they will become increasingly stressed. This stress, in turn, leads to increased cortisol production. In a dog, the urge to quickly rid themselves of the excess cortisol arises and they do this by metabolizing it through movement. This means you will have a tired dog that is at the same time hyperactive. If you don't know this background, you may think the reason your dog is overactive is because they are not exercised enough. However, the opposite is true, and the worst thing to do in this case would be to give even more exercise that drains their depleted energy reserves. Sleep deprivation leads to stress, which leads to more sleep deprivation. You are dealing with a dangerous cycle that is difficult to break. However, if you wait too long, it can quickly lead to health problems or further problematic behavior, which must be avoided at all costs. As previously noted, many dogs find it difficult to relax. They cannot just lie down and relax on command, so it is up to the owner to teach them how to regain their composure.

Now I would like to present you with some signs that your dog is overexcited but can't calm down on its own. You should not ignore this and take it as an incentive to take action yourself:

- His body is never relaxed. The muscles are constantly tense, and the ears are alertly upright.
- He makes many noises such as barking, chirping, howling or whimpering. It may sometimes happen that he starts to tremble.
- The dog may tend to impulsive behaviors that he doesn't typically show. This includes jumping on people, excessive digging and digging, or biting the leash.
- When approached, he shows little reaction and doesn't listen to you and your commands anymore.
- He appears overexcited, as if he were wide awake and wouldn't need sleep. He demands additional movement with emphasis.
- It seems as if he is not purposely ignoring you, but not perceiving you at all. This refers not only to you as a person, but also to his entire environment. Sometimes he seems disoriented and confused and can barely concentrate.
- He is constantly moving and doesn't want to sit or lie down. If he does, he doesn't stay in that position but stands up again after a short moment.
- Under certain circumstances, he may even refuse his food, which he never had enough of before.

As you can see, some of the signs are ambiguous and could indicate other problems that you should respond to with ignorance. It's not always easy to recognize the right approach. Therefore, be especially attentive when your dog exhibits behavior from one of the mentioned points. However, if it happens frequently, it is relatively clear that he is overexerted and you know how to proceed.

It's also important to note that reading this might make it seem like stress is something incredibly terrible that should always be avoided, even in the smallest amounts. It's not necessary to wrap your dog up so much that he doesn't experience any stress at all. Some stress is part of the territory. Additionally, this would interfere with your training around impulse control, as it involves exposing him to a lot of stress. Instead, focus on reducing stress together with your dog when it becomes excessive, and stay relaxed. Finally, we must not forget that our dogs pick up on our own emotions. If you're stressed and worried about him constantly, this nervousness will transfer to him and make the whole situation even more complicated.

Since this book aims not only at solutions but also at exploring the causes, I would like to introduce you to various factors that could cause restlessness. These are highly individual, so you will need to conduct some additional research to find out what stresses your dog the most.

- **Breed:** Many dog breeds that were specifically bred for activities can be difficult to imagine as calm and relaxed. Watching them in action, they seem to have an almost endless energy. Examples of this are the Husky, various Terriers, the Border Collie, and the Australian Shepherd. Caution is advised with these breeds, as there is usually a narrow margin between over- and under-stimulation. These dogs need to be moved and occupied a lot, so it would not be correct to put them under less strain as a matter of principle. A special emphasis should be placed on impulse control and frustration tolerance, as this helps in most cases. On the other hand, most smaller dog breeds are more in need of peace and easier to evaluate.

- **Age:** Of course, age also plays a decisive role in terms of the need for rest. A curious young dog with a big, wide world to explore will tire out much later than an elderly senior who is not the fittest with his 10 years. This does not mean that young dogs can run wild at will: they should especially take it easy at first and learn from the ground up that regular and long periods of rest are necessary. This will make it easier for him in the future course of training.

- **Genetics and social circumstances:** In dogs, certain personality traits and characteristics are often inherited. It may happen that puppies already carry the nervousness or at least the high probability of its expression from their mother from the start. If you stay in a social environment with her for a long time and experience this type firsthand, the puppies will probably also adopt it. This point refers not only to the mother's company, but also to the general socialization of the puppies. If it is poor, they are more susceptible to stress.

- **Daily stressors:** This refers to the everyday influences that your dog faces. There are many different stimuli that can cause stress. The screaming of small children, strange visitors, multiple dogs in the same household, an encounter with an aggressive dog during the walk. Lack of affection, very loud noises, extreme weather influences, persistent pain and illnesses also count. These are often common circumstances that can keep your dog's stress level high and prevent him from finding peace.

- **Your behavior:** As I explained earlier, dogs are affected by our nervousness. This so-called mood transfer reaches much further, so pay more attention to yourself if you don't know why your dog is currently so stressed. This does not necessarily have to refer to acute sensations - it is perfectly okay if you have a bad day and are overwhelmed. However, if there is a permanent negative mood in your household, your four-legged friend will also suffer. This includes all kinds of incidents: persistent arguments with your partner, a snippy tone in conversations, hectic due to lack of time management, worries about existence. Is there something like this with you? If so, please think about what can be done to make life together calmer for all involved.

- **The thyroid:** In dogs, a malfunction of the thyroid has far-reaching consequences. A typical side effect of hyperthyroidism is nervousness and restlessness. If there is suspicion of this, you should visit your veterinarian. A blood test will bring clarity.

- **Hyperactivity:** It is assumed that dogs can be hyperactive, but the diagnosis is much more difficult than in humans, which is why in most cases only a rough assumption can be made. It may be considered if clear behavioral differences are found compared to other dogs of the same breed and age group, which cannot be explained by character traits. If this is the case, you should see a dog behavior therapist for additional help. The following indicators could indicate this:
  - ➢ **There is little impulse control in terms of emotions:** The dog experiences his emotions or impulses especially intensely, both positive and negative. This includes the desire to play, joy, fear, and anger.

- **Frustration tolerance is insufficiently developed:** There are regular outbursts. This can go so far that the dog becomes so crazy that he even bites his owner because he does not know how to deal with the situation.
- **He lacks inhibitions with other people:** Whenever strangers or friends come into play, the dog forgets all good manners. He wants to greet them immediately and becomes agitated, jumps on them. Sometimes he can touch them, for example nudge or bump them, destroy carried objects or bark or whine at them.
- **The dog has an excessive urge to move:** This urge can also be only a side effect of hyperactivity and does not have to be triggered by stress.
- **He is very sensitive to various stimuli:** That dogs can sometimes react strongly to loud noises or the spontaneous visit of a stranger, unsecured fellow species, is normal and understandable. If your dog shows such a strong reaction to the smallest stimuli, caution is advised. He should not be frightened or disturbed by the smallest noises, for example the stirring of coffee when the spoon touches the cup. Furthermore, he could behave very restlessly at home and always stay in the area of doors or windows to keep everything in sight and to be able to perceive all new stimuli in good time. It becomes particularly difficult if he cannot remain relaxed whenever people come toward you outside. Here there could be a dangerous outburst because he wrongly assesses these people as a threat.

Tips for Daily Life

Let's move on to what you can do about it. In general, it can be said that the following options go hand in hand with training. One thing without the other makes little sense, so feel free to combine it into your daily life.

- **Music:** Music therapy is not only suitable for people but also for animals. Classical music in particular provides more peace and lowers cortisol levels. It doesn't necessarily have to be this genre; you can take advantage of your animal's conditioning. This means that certain music played during a particularly nice or relaxing moment will be associated with positive emotions by your dog in the future. For example, if you have the habit of relaxing on the couch in the evenings with a book, petting your dog and listening to your favorite music, feel free to use it. With a little luck, these good feelings are so strong that your dog will relax and find peace just from listening.

- **Natural remedies:** Adaptil and Zylkène are two substances that are wonderful natural support for relaxation. Adaptil comes in several forms: as a spray, tablets, collar, or a convenient diffuser that can easily be placed in any electrical outlet. It works in the form of pheromones, which are meant to remind the dog of the messenger substances it received from its mother's mammary glands when it was a puppy. This creates a sense of security and imitates that warm feeling. This way, your dog can relax. Zylkène also makes use of the mother's milk, or rather, its digestion. During this process, α-casozepin is produced in the puppy's gut, which enhances the effect of gamma-aminobutyric acid (GABA), a neurotransmitter. This regulates all emotions and functions, including stress, in puppies. Adult dogs no longer produce α-

casozepin, but still benefit from its effects when it is administered. They can then deal with stressful situations more easily. Zylkène is usually administered in the form of tablets. Please note that these two aids are not a permanent solution. They are suitable for stressful situations that will end soon, but will not help with chronic stress.

- **Aromatherapy Oils:** We humans enjoy the calming effects of lavender and chamomile, and these herbs and the scent of their oils are also popular with dogs. You can administer the herbs with food. Be sure to mix them in during calm phases of the dog, not during stressful ones. Otherwise, a diffuser is also suitable, but the quality of the oils is important. Make sure they are of high quality and prepared gently, and it's better to spend a little more money if in doubt.

- **Tone therapy with the RelaxoPet:** This is a device that emits specially tailored tones for our four-legged friends, which are not noticeable to us humans, so you don't have to worry about being disturbed by it. The effect is controversial. Some dog owners swear by it, while others don't notice any improvement. It has not yet been scientifically proven. If you take advantage of the conditioning, it can work well. To do this, use the RelaxoPet at first in situations where your dog is deeply relaxed. Your dog will perceive this sound as a relaxing tone, which can help in future stressful situations. Conditioning takes time and requires many repetitions to solidify the connection in the brain.

- **Fabrics for a calming touch:** Clothing for dogs may seem strange to many owners at first, but it can make sense when it comes to relaxation. There are special, close-fitting shirts or body wraps that are wrapped around the dog. By this close contact and light pressure, a touch is imitated that facilitates the dog's relaxation. It is important to test these aids in peace beforehand. Put the clothes on your dog in a relaxed situation and observe if it feels comfortable or wants to get out as quickly as possible. Only when it has become accustomed to the feeling and shows no signs of discomfort, you can begin to use it in stressful situations. Whether a calming effect will be shown, however, depends on the dog and cannot be predicted. It's definitely worth a try.

- **Create a retreat:** Almost everyone enjoys having their own little space where they can retreat during stressful situations. A place where no one disturbs them, they can do their own thing and feel truly free. Such places help us unwind and escape from everyday life whenever necessary. Your beloved companion should also have such a place in your home. Where it is and what it looks like is up to you or your dog's preferences. Some have room for a whole dog room, others choose a shady spot in the garden. It's important that he's comfortable there and can recharge. Especially in larger families where things can quickly become loud and hectic, this retreat should be located away from the main activities so the dog can escape these situations. This does not mean that he cannot be with you - if he has always been lying in the living room, he should be able to continue doing so. Just create another place for him to have peace. Furthermore, he should be able to make some decisions at this place. Allow him to take his favorite toy with him when he wants to chew on it during calm moments. Create a comfortable spot for him that he likes - if he likes the old blanket better than the new, expensive dog basket, you should allow him to have it, even if it's annoying.

- **Respect boundaries:** Another important point. If you notice that your dog is retreating and needs peace and quiet, let him have it. Please do not disturb him unless it is absolutely necessary. For example, if you want to go for a long lunchtime walk and you want to take your dog with you but he has just fallen asleep, ask yourself if he shouldn't stay at home. If you have children, please make them aware. It's especially hard for kids not to pet or play with a cute dog whenever they want. It can quickly happen that they demand too much from him and stress him out, especially if his rest times are repeatedly interrupted. Teach the children that they can play with the dog to their heart's content once he is well-rested.

- **Create structures and rules:** Creating fixed structures in daily life provides security and helps your dog relax better. It is essential for them to know that there will be a morning walk at seven o'clock, a ball game at one o'clock, food at four o'clock, and the day will end with an evening walk at seven o'clock. This way, they can plan and roughly know when they can rest without being disturbed soon. If there is no fixed routine, a certain amount of tension will always persist in the background. They will wonder when you will be home today, when they can eat, and when movement is required. Of course, it will not always be possible to stick to this schedule every day. Something may come up and these times may need to be postponed. Just try to orient yourself as often as possible.

- **Slow down your walks:** When you only have a few walks a day, the need often arises to make these as exciting and varied as possible. You take three different toys, regularly choose different routes, meet unfamiliar dogs, and play with them. Variety is not bad and your dog will be happy, but you should be careful not to overdo it. Your dog will be faced with many stimuli anyway, so it is not necessary to launch the full action program every time. Otherwise, it can quickly lead to overstimulation, which will tire your dog mentally. So try taking a slow walk in nature. Find a sprawling meadow or a small forest where you mostly have peace. If your dog runs safely without a leash and does not escape, you can safely unclip it if the environment and local regulations allow it. Otherwise, you can use a drag leash to give them the greatest possible freedom. Now you can take your time to leisurely stroll through nature. Don't think about taking your dog for a walk, but about looking at the environment together with him. If he wants to sniff a tree trunk, let him and look at a beautiful flower or the shape of the clouds while doing so. You can show each other something or let yourself be surprised where your four-legged friend takes you. Take some time with you so that you don't feel rushed and can adopt a relaxed pace. Walk slowly and stop when you want. It may take your dog some time to get used to it and get impatient relatively quickly. In this case, stick to your usual pace and only occasionally include slower phases, which can be extended each time. You will see that, over time, your dog will appreciate these phases more and more.

- **Incorporate the ceiling exercise into your training** (ceiling training - so your dog can relax anywhere, 2022): The beauty of this exercise is that it is suitable for absolutely any dog. Don't be afraid of it; the earlier you start, the better. It teaches the dog to ease the waiting in stressful situations so that he doesn't remain on edge until it continues/ends. This exercise should only be performed when your dog is relatively calm and has a clear head, otherwise he won't be able to acquire what he has learned. The optimal training conditions exist when he is physically and mentally exhausted and has had a chance to calm down after this effort. You will need the following things:

A collar with a leash, alternatively a harness and a small blanket or mat that is only used for this exercise. In the future, you will take this blanket with you and be able to provide calm on the go, so pay attention to its ease of handling. The reason why this exercise is so successful is the blanket itself: it creates a spatial boundary and defines a fixed area that the dog will automatically associate with calm. Your aid: conditioning. To avoid distorting this or linking the wrong stimulus, additional rewards such as treats are omitted. The actual reward consists exclusively of the dog being able to calm down.

This is how it is practiced:

Let's move on to the exercise. Find a spot in your home where you will place the unused blanket. This place should be in a corner or another convenient location where the distance from doors, windows, and people is large. This creates a reduced risk of distractions during the exercise. The dog is leashed and then led to the blanket. You can introduce the command "blanket" here if you like. Now wait until the dog lies down on it or sits on it by itself. Finally, turn away from the dog. Whenever the dog stands up again, repeat the entire process. Continue until the dog stays lying down, even if you move away and don't return right away. Over time, the dog should learn to relax when you are doing your own tasks, no matter where they are. This exercise takes a lot of time, especially in the beginning. Repeat it as often as needed until the desired result is achieved. The exercise is finished when you are satisfied and only when you have explicitly allowed the dog to leave the blanket. Make sure the dog leaves calmly and doesn't run away frantically. The rest time should not be seen as a punishment that should end as soon as possible.

To increase the training, gradually increase the distance. First, turn away from it and stay in your position. Next time, take one step further, then two. If the dog gets up, go back and guide him back to the blanket. Even if you're already at the other end of the room, go directly to him and don't try to send him back to his spot from that distance. Especially stubborn or clever dogs could take this as a challenge and try to undermine your authority through arguments or misbehavior. Don't give them the opportunity and make it clear from the beginning that there is no other option to complete this exercise. The leash can help you guide him back more easily and prevent him from escaping, even if he wants to.

Once you're confident that he will stay lying down, you can start to do simple tasks or activities while still keeping an eye on him. Do something relaxed that doesn't require you to move much around the room and make the dog curious. Read a book, wash dishes, etc. If he can relax well during this time, you can gradually increase it until you can do whatever you want. The most important thing is to be consistent and patient.

If you successfully master this task, you can gradually increase the stimuli by moving the training outside. If you have a garden, you can start there since the environment is familiar. Otherwise, you can take your blanket with you anywhere, even to friends or cafes and restaurants. This way, your furry friend will remain calm and relaxed in exciting environments. Make sure that the people you spend time with are respectful of the training. Even though it's tempting for your dog to sit quietly next to you and let you pet him, he should be ignored by everyone present. The blanket remains his resting area, where he should not be disturbed!

Conditioned Relaxation

We have previously discussed that conditioning can be a very helpful tool in terms of relaxation. Now I would like to delve deeper into this topic and explain the basics of conditioned relaxation, regardless of the respective influences (Blaschke-Berthold, 2020).

Basically, it can be said that the brain decides between two opposing processes or states, namely excitement and relaxation. Depending on which state prevails in the dog, its reactions to environmental stimuli and its behavior are different. The more excited it is, the more intensely it experiences negative emotions like anger and fear, which in turn leads to problematic behavior. That's why a lot of attention has to be paid to relaxation, as only it can help to lower the excitement level. The problem is that relaxation is not easy to control. In some situations, we simply don't have the time or the right quiet environment to calm our dog down quickly. Nevertheless, there is a tool with conditioning that can help us quickly turn the situation around in such cases.

Now some background on the processes within the brain: A certain area of the brainstem plays a major role here, namely the Formatio Reticularis. This is a network of neurons that transmits information from various areas and thus controls important functions. This includes the regulation of states of attention and activity. More specifically, there are two core states, the thinking and the reflexive. In the thinking state, the animal is conscious and independently seeks solutions to problems. In the reflexive state, instincts take over and the animal acts solely on the basis of automatic reactions. It can hardly influence this behavior itself and even less can this behavior be suppressed from the outside. This state is vital for survival, as it triggers a fight-or-flight reaction that can be decisive in dangerous situations. However, it should remain that way, as this would mean more potential sources of danger in everyday life. Such severe reactions rarely end well, so it is important to ensure that your dog remains in the thinking state for most of its time. The problem: The higher the arousal level, the more likely the Formatio Reticularis will switch the dog to change its state. To prevent this or make it revert back as quickly as possible, we use a hormone: Oxytocin. This hormone is primarily responsible for strengthening social bonds and promoting relaxation. The simplest and most direct way to increase the release of oxytocin is through the skin. Gentle stimulation, such as stroking, warmth, and light vibrations, activate certain fibers that interpret this stimulus as a pleasant touch and thus increase the production of this hormone. We can easily take care of it ourselves to make our dog feel more comfortable. We now take advantage of this fact using classical conditioning. This associates an external stimulus with a physiological reaction.

The most well-known example of this is Pavlov's dog:

- When the dog is presented with a bowl of food, the stimulus, its salivation, the response, is triggered.
- The food is gone. Now the bell, the neutral stimulus, comes into play. Ringing the bell doesn't elicit any special response from the dog.
- The food comes back and the salivation is triggered again. Meanwhile, the ringing of the bell stimulus is added. Salivation is an unconditioned response.
- With enough repetition, the dog has learned that the ringing of the bell, the conditioned stimulus, must have something to do with the delicious food. From now on, every time the bell rings,

the conditioned response of salivation will be automatically triggered, even if there is no food in front of it.

This schema could be applied to any stimuli. Here we want to use it to couple a signal word with the physiological relaxation response using a stimulus. Here are the steps to follow:

1. Find out what makes your furry friend really relax. Pay attention to the best possible stimulation of the skin - stroke, massage, or brush your dog with a soft, gentle brush. Experiment over the course of several days to determine the best way. It's important that the corresponding touch can relax him within seconds, not after an hour. You'll recognize when this state sets in: First, the area of the spine relaxes and the tail is lowered. Then comes the face, the muscles relax, and he will have a dreamy look. After that, he will typically lie on his side. Once you've found a way to quickly and reliably trigger this response, continue to step 2.
2. From now on, your signal word comes into play, for example, "calm." Always say the word first before touching the dog. This is the stimulus you want to condition. Immediately after, start with the unconditioned stimulus, the touch, which in turn triggers the physiological process, the relaxation with simultaneous oxytocin release.
3. With sufficient repetitions, the signal word becomes a conditioned stimulus and triggers relaxation without physical touch.
4. The work is far from done here. From now on, the conditioned stimulus must be reinforced and confirmed to ensure that it can be reliably applied. Whenever your dog is completely relaxed, repeat the signal word multiple times. Later, it will help to calm him down when physical touch is no longer effective.

It is important to note that conditioned relaxation is not a miracle cure that will automatically make the dog lie down and become calm in the most exciting situations. It is simply a means of returning him from a reflexive to a thinking state and influencing him through commands or other tactics to calm down further. Essentially, it is the safety net that can save you in most cases when nothing else works. If that is not possible, then you should remove the dog from the situation as soon as possible and not expose him to the disturbing stimuli any longer.

That all sounds logical and easy, but there are some pitfalls to watch out for in conditioning training in order to be successful:

- Don't get hung up on a particular training approach. Just because the pairing of touch and relaxation works for most dogs doesn't mean it will work for all. If you don't see a connection after many training sessions, it's unlikely that one will develop. This doesn't necessarily mean you made errors in training. Some dogs can't relax through touch, whether due to negative experiences such as abuse, chronic pain, or simply because it's not in their nature. Take this into account! Find another stimulus that relaxes your dog. Your dog should feel comfortable during training, otherwise it's useless.

- If you are too rigid and tense in your behavior, your dog will notice. During training, you are focused and attentive. You want to observe your dog's reaction precisely and record progress. It is logical that this expectation and concentration are reflected in your gaze. The problem is that your dog picks up on this look. It may be that he feels pressured by it and cannot relax. After all, he does not know what you expect from him at that moment and what he should do since conditioning is a process of the subconscious. Imagine trying to relax while constantly being stared at. Not very pleasant. Therefore, during exercises, be completely relaxed. Treat petting like a casual activity. Focus on yourself and relax, and this will make it easier for your dog too.

- Conditioning doesn't always go in one direction. If you use the relaxation cue in stressful situations too often, your dog may eventually associate it with a state of arousal, which renders the conditioned relaxation ineffective. This doesn't mean it has to happen. You can counteract this by continually reinforcing the relaxation cue. Stay on top of it, ideally several times a day. Get into the habit of using the cue automatically during relaxed moments.

- Don't approach the matter with exaggerated expectations. As already mentioned, conditioned relaxation is not a miracle cure. It cannot prevent your dog's arousal level from rising, especially in exciting situations such as walks. This means that you must always apply it in combination with other problem-solving strategies. When the dog leaves the reflexive state and returns to the thinking state, his brain needs an incentive to think. You can't just leave him hanging. It would be like this situation: You're doing something because you think it's right in that moment. Suddenly someone comes around the corner and says, "Stop right now, that's not how it's done!" Now you're in this situation and have to do something to move forward, but you don't know what to do. "What should I do?" you would ask yourself. If there is no answer to that, you would feel overwhelmed and helpless. Therefore, it is important to give the dog guidance.

Let's look at an example with playing:

You take a trip to the dog park because you're meeting a friend and their dog, who is a playmate for your four-legged friend. In such situations, your dog is so aroused that he acts reflexively.

As soon as you unleash him, he sprints off uncontrollably and almost knocks over his friend. Since you don't like this behavior, you have taught him conditioned relaxation. When you arrive at the park, you notice how your dog's arousal level increases. He becomes restless, pulls on the leash, and wags his tail very excitedly. He doesn't listen to normal commands like "sit" and "down" anymore. You use the relaxation word and notice that he becomes clearer again and looks at you for a change. Say "sit" again and release him once he complies. Then let him sit briefly and wait until he has calmed down. After that, give him the release command "let's go" and he can run to his friend and play with him. This way you have shown him that he can still greet him and play with him extensively, but only when he is calm.

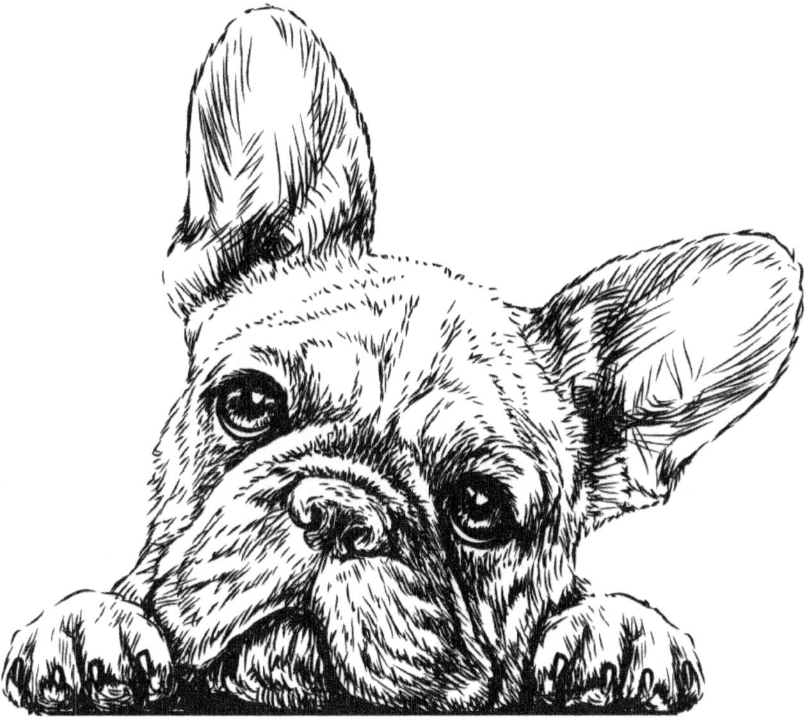

THEORETICAL FOUNDATIONS FOR TRAINING

In order to ensure that your dog takes away all the important information from the practical exercises later on, we first deal with how his learning process works. You probably know it from school: With a teacher who responded to his students and adapted his teaching style to them, you could understand the material much easier and retain it in the long term. Therefore, in dog training, the following applies: If your dog is to become a good student, you must become a good teacher.

How do dogs learn?

How do dogs learn in the first place? To understand this, we turn to learning theory. This is not pure speculation, but biological processes within the brain that are scientifically proven. It is inherent in every dog, regardless of breed, age, or how well trained they are. This is one of the few things that you only have to memorize once and that always works in the same way without having to determine additional factors. Since learning theory is also one of the most important foundations for dealing with your beloved friend, this knowledge will greatly facilitate all further steps.

Let's start with the most important question: What is learning? Learning is a lifelong process in which our behavior patterns change based on our experiences. It allows living beings to adapt to all adversities and avoid repeating the same mistake multiple times. From this, one can deduce the goal: optimizing one's own behavior. Learning enables us to minimize damage while pursuing the satisfaction of our needs. For us humans, the objective could be formulated as follows: "How do I best approach a potential partner to convince them of me?" or "How do I move my car through traffic to quickly reach my destination without endangering myself and others?". For a dog, the goals may be simpler. They could be, for example, "Where can I find the most restful sleeping place?" or "How can I play with the cat without being attacked?". You see that the basic principle is identical. Learning helps us explore our environment and adapt to it.

There isn't just one form of learning, but many subtypes that are difficult to list in their entirety. Therefore, I would like to introduce to you the forms that are used in working with dogs:

- **Classical conditioning.**

- **Operant conditioning** (The various forms of learning in dogs | Animalia, n.d.): It works differently from classical conditioning, such as in the case of conditioned relaxation. We use various stimuli again, but they are used as reinforcement or punishment to induce a conscious change in behavior. There are both positive and negative reinforcements and punishments. They work as follows:

The dog shows unwanted behavior by repeatedly chewing on your shoes and destroying them, even in your presence.

- **Positive reinforcement:** A pleasant stimulus is added, such as a treat. This rewards the dog for staying near the shoes and not touching them.
- **Negative reinforcement:** An unpleasant stimulus is removed. For example, if you previously scolded him energetically when he destroyed your shoes, he now realizes that the scolding is absent when he refrains from this behavior, which causes relief in him.
- **Positive punishment:** An unpleasant consequence is created. Whenever your dog does something to the shoes, he is punished. An example of this would be locking him out.
- **Negative punishment:** A pleasant stimulus is taken away. This would be the case, for example, if you take away his favorite toy.

Reinforcements are meant to increase the likelihood of a certain behavior occurring, while punishments are meant to minimize it. Note that operant conditioning should be used with caution. Punishments are rarely effective with dogs, as they create double the work. They learn which behavior to avoid, but not which behavior is desired. Reinforcements or rewards are better in this case. If you promote the desired behavior, the undesired behavior will decrease at the same time, killing two birds with one stone.

It is also important to note that operant conditioning never works retroactively. Neither rewards nor punishments make sense if they are used hours after the behavior occurred. You only have a few seconds to relate the reinforcement or punishment to the shown behavior. This means that if you come home from work and are upset that your new pair of shoes has been destroyed, punishment will not help - no matter how upset you are. If you then punish your dog for it, he will not understand what he did wrong at that point. This would in turn create negative emotions, building additional frustration.

Have you thought about continuing to reward your dog for following commands, even if he has been doing it reliably for years? Many dog owners are happy when the training is finally over and take it for granted that their four-legged friend listens to them. However, you can assume operant conditioning here again: By removing the positive stimulus of praise, treats, or other rewards, you indirectly show the dog that this behavior, i.e., following commands, is no longer desired. If you're unlucky, the dog can quickly unlearn this behavior. Of course, you don't have to use rewards as meticulously as before, but regular appreciation is definitely appropriate.

- **Habituation** (*The different types of learning in dogs | Animalia*, n.d.): Here, we are talking about "habituation." The goal is to teach the dog not to react to certain stimuli. This is particularly useful for stressed and anxious dogs, as it allows for the elimination of an annoying stimulus. For example, let's say the dog is generally afraid of loud noises and can't stand it when you vacuum. You can lead him step by step to the solution. He is afraid of the combination of the vacuum cleaner and the noise it makes. Start with the device: for example, you can initially place the vacuum cleaner in the room where your dog often stays. Then push it through the apartment as if you were really vacuuming, but leave it turned off. Since no noise is produced, the dog learns that the vacuum cleaner itself is not bad. Now you can gradually increase the stimulation by turning on the device at the lowest setting and working up to the normal setting over time. This way, the dog gets used to the noise and will be able to cope with it in the future. This applies not only to noise but to all kinds of stimuli. They are carefully dosed, so the dog no longer has to be afraid of them when they occur in their full extent.

- **Spatial learning:** One of the most important forms of learning for any living being. The animal perceives itself and the characteristics of its surroundings, such as distance, size, and texture. The dog learns if it's big enough to jump on the sofa, to avoid the edge of the table in time, having hit it a few times and felt pain, and to take a wide berth around the pond while running in the garden because it cannot walk on water and will fall in. The goal is to be able to safely orient oneself and move around in the space.

- **Temporal learning:** Even though dogs cannot read a clock, they still learn about time. As they age, they internalize important times, such as when they will be fed or taken for a walk and are ready on the dot. They also understand important concepts such as day and night, knowing that they should sleep at night and move around during the day when they feel like it.

- **Sensitization** (*The different forms of learning in dogs | Animalia*, n.d.): This type of learning behavior is rather negative and associated with additional stress for the animal. It is the opposite of habituation: the reaction to the respective stimulus does not decrease over time, but instead becomes more intense. For stressed dogs, this means additional fear when the stimulus occurs again. If the dog is startled every time the neighbors' children scream, it can get worse and worse. Sensitization may occur in conjunction with habituation. This means that although the dog will continue to be frightened, the more often the children scream, the more accustomed he will become to it. If the stimulus is changed - even if only slightly - habituation may have to start anew. This would be the case, for example, if the children not only screamed but also threw a ball against the wall, which produces additional noise. Be careful if you want to use habituation: if you do this too quickly and do not give the dog enough time to get used to it, several weeks are a must, he can quickly become overwhelmed by the stimulus, and the whole thing can turn into unwanted sensitization.

- **Learning by insight:** One of the simplest forms of learning. It is used when the dog has tried something specific several times and has come to a rock-solid result. For example, if he used to fit through the cat flap, he will continue to try - simply on principle, because he does not know how much he has grown. At some point, he will no longer fit through it. Nevertheless, he will not give up and try it a few more times, just to come to the conclusion again that it no longer works. After this trial-and-error phase, insight eventually comes, that he will never fit through the cat flap again and has to find another way into the garden. Once he has come to this realization, he will never try this behavior again.

- **Social learning:** (*The different forms of learning in dogs | Animalia*, n.d.) Dogs are very social animals, so they acquire a large part of their knowledge about their own kind or humans. In this form of learning, it usually concerns places or objects that only arouse the dog's special interest when someone else is involved in it. For example, your four-legged friend will hardly be interested in a passing butterfly – if it lands near you and you approach it to take a look, it will not be long before your dog suddenly stands next to you and does the same thing.

- **Imitation** (*The Different Forms of Learning in Dogs | Animalia*, n.d.): This type of learning is very similar to social learning, but it refers more to specific behaviors that are adopted from others. When it comes to opening a door, your dog will eventually internalize that you press down the handle and then push the door forward. He will try the same thing by jumping up, using his paw to press the handle, and shifting his weight forward. Similarly, he will want to taste the food that you always enjoy.

- **Imprinting** (*Puppy Socialization and Imprinting | n.d.*): It is an essential part of a puppy's socialization. Puppies should be extensively imprinted on various stimuli during the first few months of life. They should be allowed to meet unfamiliar people and dogs, explore new environments, ride in cars, and much more. Essentially, imprinting is the first contact with different stimuli that shows him that he doesn't need to be afraid and is prepared for any situation. It creates a great sense of self-confidence, trust in the owner, and the environment, which makes the dog more confident and less prone to developing fears later in life.

- **Fear conditioning:** It works like classical conditioning, but in a negative context. In this case, the corresponding stimulus triggers fear and stress in the dog, which is why this learning process must be avoided. Let's take a look at the previous example of chewed shoes:

Mr. Schmidt loves expensive shoes and regularly sets aside money to treat himself to a nice new pair every few months. He has recently gotten his first puppy, who is very curious and not yet well-trained due to his young age. One day, Mr. Schmidt comes home to find that a pair of shoes has been completely ruined. His dog lies calmly beside them and looks at him innocently. Mr. Schmidt takes a deep breath, swallows his frustration, and puts the shoes away. He hopes that this was just a one-time occurrence. A few days later, when he finds the next pair of shoes in pieces, he gets upset and scolds his dog. However, the puppy's behavior does not stop and the incidents begin to accumulate. Eventually, Mr. Schmidt becomes so upset that he hits his dog out of anger. This happens so often that the dog eventually expects violence when his owner comes home from work – even when he is no longer interested in shoes and there is no reason for Mr. Schmidt to be angry with him. The fear conditioning triggers the dog to cower in a distant corner instead of happily greeting his owner. The dog doesn't know why his human did that. It can go so far that he generally fears his owner, avoids him altogether, or even bites him to keep further harm away. This type of learning should not be underestimated as it is very difficult to reverse.

- **Taste aversion learning** (Oberli, 2022): This is a form of learning that can quickly become dangerous. It occurs when a dog eats something and, for whatever reason, does not tolerate it. Perhaps the dog was playing too vigorously, its stomach was still full, and after eating a carrot, it vomits it up afterwards. Although the carrot itself is not to blame and would even taste very good to him under other circumstances, it can happen that he develops an aversion to it, that he may not want to eat it again for a certain period of time or even never again. Not only vomiting is a trigger for this, but also pain or digestive problems can be the cause. This can be limited to individual foods, but in the worst case, the dog may not want to eat anything at all.

- **Discrimination learning:** In this form, the dog learns to distinguish between different things. This happens through different senses, such as feeling the texture with the tongue, taste, appearance, hearing, and so on. Through the various impressions, the dog learns that there are many different objects in its environment and that some things are not the same, even though they may look very similar. This is one of the basic skills and is firmly established early on, but can also be very useful. The dog can not only navigate its environment better but also avoid potential sources of danger. For example, if a poison bait is laid out in the form of a sausage, it can help if the dog sniffs it and realizes that something is wrong based on a different scent. Of course, factors such as self-control come into play here, and it is not guaranteed that the dog will not still devour the bait. Nevertheless, a well-developed discrimination learning can be the deciding factor, even in the worst-case scenario where it can be a matter of life and death.

Let's move on to the next point that plays an important role in learning: The right prerequisites must be met. These are the following three points:

1. **Intelligence.** This factor is undisputed, as it is almost always present. Of course, there are different degrees of intelligence, but every dog is intelligent and thus meets the requirement for learning. This is given when the dog responds sensibly to new and unfamiliar situations and asks itself, "How do I best deal with this now?". Furthermore, our four-legged friends possess a high degree of social intelligence, as they are capable of

building complex relationships. This applies to both dogs among themselves and other species. As long as the animal does not suffer from any other impairments, no owner needs to worry that their dog is not intelligent enough to be fully trained.

2. **Motivation.** Similar to us humans, dogs need to be motivated in order to learn well. Both internal factors, in the form of needs that need to be fulfilled, and external factors, such as environmental influences, provide them with the reasons to exhibit a certain behavior and pursue goals. If a dog sees a fleeing cat, the motivation to chase it is triggered. If a full bowl of food is placed in front of him, the motivation to eat arises. Dogs can be motivated in various ways, which can be used to your advantage as a pet owner. You need to be able to motivate your dog and thus move him to learn – on the other hand, negative influences such as the use of pressure, violence or similar would be the only alternative. However, this ultimately only indicates overwhelm and lack of knowledge, destroys the bond with the animal, and in most cases would not be effective since the dog does not feel comfortable during training. Here, once again, your powers of observation, creativity, and flexibility are called for.

3. **The Comfort Factor.** In order for the dog to be able and willing to learn, a relaxed and pleasant training atmosphere must be created. Avoid negative feelings or a high level of excitement, both in yourself and in the dog. Train in peace, with a calm mind and without time or expectation pressure. Furthermore, stimuli from the environment should be kept as low as possible, if they would bother or distract the dog. If dealing with them is not explicitly part of the training plan, you should ensure that there are not too many other people or animals present and

that the noise level is as low as possible. This way, your dog can fully concentrate on you. What is important: You must definitely take into account your four-legged friend's physical well-being. An exhausting training would be irresponsible if he is in pain or has to make an extraordinary effort for it (in view of a difficult health condition). For example, if he has problems with his hip, the "down" exercise, in which he has to lie down and get up several times during a short period of time, would be anything but pleasant.

To briefly summarize under what circumstances dogs generally learn best (*Learning theory: How does a dog learn - Part 1/5, 2017*):

- The dog is in an environment where he feels relaxed, safe, and comfortable. This includes his health, you as a training partner, and the environment in general.
- He learns in a context-specific manner and through the use of mental images. This occurs through associations, which brings us back to conditioning. He remembers certain influences and emotions in their context, and a later connection outside of this original situation is not possible.
- Dogs generalize very quickly, especially when it comes to negative experiences. If he was once very painfully injured by a cat, he may connect this pain in the future with the sight of cats in general - regardless of whether it is the same animal or another that just wants to play with him.
- They learn through play. When it comes to getting to know new objects or fellow canines, playful interactions are often used. They sniff, nudge, lick, and frolic around. Rules of behavior are usually taught playfully among dogs. They interact in a way that feels best for them and test their limits in the process. Whenever one of the animals howls, growls, or bares its teeth, it signals to the other that it has gone too far and the game is

now over. This behavior is usually never shown again, which speaks to the effectiveness of the learning process.
- Many repetitions are needed until the learned behavior is really established. Like with us humans, no one is born a master, and it cannot be assumed that only a few repetitions will lead to permanent results. One must stay on the ball, but be careful not to overwhelm the dog. Be sure to take adequate breaks between training sessions if they occur several times a day. In general, 8,000 to 10,000 repetitions are considered necessary.
- Dogs learn best in small steps. Overexertion is not only risked by practicing too often in a very short period of time, but also if the training goals are too ambitious. Choose smaller individual steps so that your dog can cope better. Make the communication and signals as clear as possible so that he always knows exactly what is being demanded of him.
- Dogs learn throughout their entire life – from puppyhood to seniority and even 24 hours a day. Of course, it is most sensible to start as early as possible and introduce the puppy to as many influences as possible to make things easier for him and you. Even old dogs are very trainable and can change their behavior, so you have nothing to fear. As far as the time of day is concerned, you don't have to pay attention to anything special. One thing that could help you, though, is to conduct a short training session in the evening before it's time for a good night's sleep. This way, your dog can work on and internalize what he learned right after and make the training twice as effective.
- Learning through rewards and punishments is the most effective method, as it has the highest motivational factor: "I want to have something./I want to avoid something or achieve that it stops." Please note my previous warnings in this regard.

- Proper use of praise is crucial. Dogs need rewards to feel valued and to recognize that their efforts were not in vain. However, too much praise is counterproductive as it has an inflationary effect. If the dog realizes that it will be praised regardless of whether it makes an effort or just barely meets your criteria, the incentive to improve will eventually disappear. Therefore, provide variety and regularly control yourself.
- Motivation also needs to be measured. We have already established that too little motivation leads to no results. If motivation is too high, the result is the same. If you have a very hungry dog in front of you who is going to be rewarded with treats afterward and already smells them, it will focus so much on the food that it won't be able to concentrate properly on the actual exercise. Always make sure that all needs are satisfied in advance.

Let's talk about the individual processes that can take place during learning. The following three processes are distinguished: non-associative learning, associative learning, and extinction, also known as "unlearning" (*Learning Theory: Most Important Learning Processes - Part 2/5, 2015*).

Non-associative learning:

This is the subconscious form of learning, in which a certain stimulus is repeated and, as a result, a behavioral change is triggered to deal with it as effectively as possible. This change occurs through the adaptation of the dog's response strength, as is the case with either habituation, attenuation, or sensitization, reinforcement. As previously determined, habituation is always to be aimed for, as this learning process saves the dog a lot of energy and time that he would otherwise unnecessarily have to spend on reacting to the respective stimulus.

Associative Learning:

This process, which works through associations, can occur both consciously and subconsciously. This includes operant and classical conditioning.

Extinction:

This process is not about learning, but about unlearning certain behaviors that were previously trained using conditioning. Such extinction does not occur suddenly, but the desired behavior decreases if the corresponding association is no longer reinforced. In the two types of conditioning, extinction works slightly differently:

- In classical conditioning, extinction occurs when the time interval between the two stimuli increases. As mentioned earlier, you don't have much time with your dog to establish a clear association between two stimuli, usually only a few seconds. Taking the example of Pavlov's dog, who associates the ringing of a bell with food and thereby triggers salivation. Once the stimulus is conditioned, the dog starts drooling just from the sound of the bell. If the regular reminder that the ringing is related to food does not occur, the process will eventually regress. The dog will forget this and eventually the bell will just be a bell. In between, the dog must be exposed to both stimuli at the same time again and again.
- In operant conditioning, extinction occurs when the desired or feared consequence of the behavior does not occur. In this case, the dog loses motivation to maintain this behavior if he gets nothing or is not punished for it. For the dog, it becomes more attractive to show another behavior - either on principle or out of curiosity.

Reward vs. Punishment - what do you have to consider?

Let's take a closer look at operant conditioning and how to apply it most effectively in dog training. We want to bring several factors under one roof: our training style should not only be successful but also animal welfare-compliant and not harmful to the dog, both physically and psychologically. Therefore, never resort to punishment before thinking about the background and carefully considering it.

First, I want to give you a few additional examples of the different types of rewards and punishments:

- **Positive reinforcement:** In this method, a distinction is made between primary and secondary reinforcers. Primary reinforcers are the immediate fulfillment of the dog's basic needs, such as playing, sleeping, eating, bathing, and mating, if desired. Secondary reinforcers work through these needs and are announced in advance through other training methods such as clicker training or verbal praise. It is important that this has already been fully conditioned. This is a globally appreciated and highly successful training method, as the desired behavior is clearly identified and rewarded under all circumstances.
- **Negative reinforcement:** In order to use negative reinforcement effectively, it is necessary to first put the dog in an unpleasant situation that is then relieved. Therefore, one should ask oneself whether it is really justifiable to deliberately harm the dog, just so that it can learn from this relief. I would like to remind you that the dog needs a certain level of comfort in order to learn effectively. Another example would be training for "sit," in which you push the dog's hindquarters down with your hand, creating an unpleasant pressure. If the dog

exhibits the desired behavior and stays sitting, the reward is given by removing your hand.

- **Positive Punishment:** Another training method that violates the individual learning requirements, as it triggers a number of negative emotions in the dog. This means that you can never achieve such effective training with punishments as with rewards. Apart from being morally questionable, there is a high hurdle that must be met for the punishment to make sense. For the dog to learn something sustainable from it, the following must be given:
  - **The punishment must occur immediately in order to be properly linked.** This alone is difficult, since the dog rarely shows problematic behavior in your presence.
  - **The punishment must occur every time the behavior is shown, without exception.** Not just behind closed doors, but also in the midst of a crowd, if necessary. Can you justify the chosen punishment in front of many curious eyes?
  - **The punishment must be strong enough to permanently prevent the behavior.** This requires a very narrow margin. A punishment that is too lenient would have no effect, while one that is too harsh would scare the dog and thus ruin your bond permanently. In addition, there is a risk of violating animal protection laws, and it should not be in a owner's interest to mistreat their dog.
  - **The punishment may only be linked to the behavior and nothing else.** We have already looked at how easy it is to condition dogs. Accordingly, it can quickly happen that two stimuli are linked together, although this was not planned. In order for the punishment to be associated as you intend, you must ensure that no other stimulus creeps into this equation. The dog must not associate the punishment with

you, other people, animals, smells or sounds under any circumstances, as this can lead to additional aversions or fears that will bring further problems.

Ask yourself if you can juggle all of these points – and that with every single punishment, not just once. You would be taking a big risk and probably do more harm than good. There is always a solution that can be achieved with rewards or other strategies.

However, there will hardly be any pet owners who have not applied positive punishment to their dogs at least once. It doesn't always have to be blows or minutes-long tirades: it would also count if you are so stressed that you react to an invitation to play with an angry "NO!" or jerk the leash abruptly when your furry friend wants to sniff a suspected poison bait. Your dog will forgive you for such slips, don't worry – as long as they are not part of your daily routine, it's okay.

- **Negative punishment:** Negative punishment is not as severe as positive punishment, but it still triggers negative emotions such as disappointment, which can accumulate as frustration. Therefore, it should be used with caution and only after careful consideration. After all, a certain expectation or hope is aroused that is disappointed when we intentionally remove the reward. Timing is crucial here. For example, if your dog jumps up on you because he wants you to play with him, and you want to stop this behavior, you should immediately turn away from him and ignore him, thereby denying him the attention he is hoping for. When he calms down on his own, sits down, or stands normally again, you should reward him by praising him and giving him the valuable attention. This is a positive reward that shows him that calm behavior is more rewarding than jumping up. He is shown which behavior to avoid, and the correction for the desired behavior follows directly after. However, if you miss the right timing, negative punishment will not work. If you react too late with your ignorance and are tempted to give him a little attention right after jumping up, the punishment is invalid because he has already gotten what he wants. If you then turn away from him, it appears as if you have some other problem with him or are arbitrarily ignoring him, which he cannot understand – frustration builds up. Depending on how well his frustration tolerance is developed, this can quickly become dangerous if these negative emotions manifest in aggressive behavior.

By the way, some people believe that with "especially difficult dogs," punishment, especially with violence, is the last resort available to them if nothing else works. This assumption is simply false, there is no dog that cannot learn with positive methods. No dog deserves to be judged based on its breed and "deserves" to be treated with less love and respect. Especially not if he is already under extreme stress or very scared, which exacerbates the problematic behavior. You now know the psychological basics and know what approach achieves what effect. Please do not be swayed by the opinions of such self-proclaimed experts (*Learning Theory: Positive and Negative Reinforcement - Part 3/5*, 2016).

Rewarding Correctly

We have looked at the effectiveness of rewards, and I urge you to primarily work with this method. Therefore, I would like to focus specifically on how you can best reward your dog and what to consider.

There is a greater variety of options than the classics like food and toys. Every dog has individual preferences in this regard, which are not set in stone. Depending on the training situation, he may want a different reward. Although he will be happy, you will have greater success if you don't just give him a treat on principle, but think about what he would like instead. I have already mentioned some possibilities before, but there are others that are not so obvious: For some dogs, the optimal reward is being allowed to sniff something, rolling around as they please, yes, even in the middle of the dirt, being able to lie in the shade during heat, shredding an old cardboard box, carrying something around, or just running.

So that you don't have to guess what types of rewards your dog likes best, you should make a list. Observe his behavior - what does he like to do most when nothing is being demanded of him? What really makes him happy? Write down possible rewards and eliminate those that don't lift him up. If you have a closer selection, try them out when the opportunity arises. This way, you won't have a free choice in the situation where a reward is due, but, for example, three or four options. This will make it much easier for you to make the right choice.

When the opportunity is set, there are several options. If the treat is chosen, you should find out which food your dog prefers for it. Some dogs are content with a piece of kibble, others are happy with a piece of sausage, while others prefer a premium snack. Test his preference in a neutral situation by presenting him with several options. The one that the dog wants to eat first is best suited as a reward.

Learning to choose the best option depending on the situation is not as difficult as it sounds. Dogs are very predictable in this regard, and so are we humans. Imagine you are a child again and want to go on an exciting canoe trip with your best friend. Now your mother says no and hands you a sandwich that is filled just the way you like it. Of course, you're happy about the sandwich, but it's not what you were hoping for in that moment. It's clear what would have been appropriate instead: either the canoe trip or an alternative activity that would have been even better. Therefore, always pay attention to the context in which you practice with your dog. The reward is always based on the unwanted behavior that he should stop. It should show him that he would have more of it if he acted differently. This only works if your alternative reward is better. This means that if he is not supposed to sniff or eat something disgusting, a treat is appropriate. If he is not supposed to run too excitedly towards his playmate, an intense play session is due afterwards. If he is not supposed to chase after any animals, then tire him out afterwards by throwing a ball or playing tug-of-war with him.

It makes sense that the reward varies depending on the performance achieved. You should always have an ace up your sleeve that is of higher value than the regular reward, such as "normal" toys and one that makes noise or dry food and several pieces of sausage with cheese. Whenever he has performed exceptionally well, shown desired behavior after many attempts for the first time, or finally overcome his stubbornness regarding a problem, he deserves such a special reward. For other things that he has mastered, the usual type is sufficient. You don't need to use something special only when he has achieved something for the first time as you want it. It can also serve as a wonderful motivation during the learning process whenever a significant progress is observed for the first time.

Regarding petting and stroking as a reward, it is only partially useful. There will be dogs who really enjoy it, but for most, it is not desirable in this context. Pay attention to his body language to find out how he feels about it. If you can't judge his reaction clearly, then simply compare it, for example, to the use of treats or toys and draw your conclusions from that.

An important fact on the side note: Even if you have an unambiguously strong bond with your dog, he does not do anything out of pure love for you - that is wishful thinking. He will not sit down whenever you want him to just to make you happy. Rather, this behavior always happens out of the motivation to gain an advantage for himself. So you can see why it is so important to always offer an incentive in the form of a reward. However, it becomes a bit more difficult, as rewards should not be used arbitrarily. This is where the so-called reinforcement schedules come into play, which define the further course of action. There are interval and ratio reinforcement. Both options can be applied either intermittently or constantly, that is, variable or continuous.

A continuous reinforcement, that is, a constant one, is useful when new behavior is to be learned, as it continuously increases the likelihood of its occurrence. Variable reinforcement adds variety to the mix and ensures that previously learned behavior is not so susceptible to extinction. If you want the dog to reliably follow a certain behavior that you value highly, it must be highly rewarded every time - even the thousandth time (*Learning theory: Positive reinforcement, how to do it - Part 4/5, 2016*).

Applying the Learning Theory Correctly

Before we move on to further practical exercises, I would like to explain how to apply the theory in the best way possible. Each training session should be well-prepared and adapted to your dog's needs. The following points should be considered (*Learning Theory: Applied Correctly in Dog Training - Part 5/5, 2016*):

- What are the dog's characteristics, such as breed, age, gender, and health?
- What learning phase is he in?
- What learning forms and techniques do you want to use?

- What goal do you want to achieve?
- What type and quality of rewards should be used?

The learning phases:

Dogs go through four learning phases, each of which flows seamlessly into the next. At the beginning is the "acquisition phase". New behavior is established by reinforcing the desired behavior through rewards. Two techniques are available: luring and shaping.

Luring involves using all kinds of means, such as toys and food, to encourage the dog to do something without coercion and of its own accord. In most cases, these are initially held in the hand. Once the dog understands the desired behavior, this lure must be gradually removed – the goal is for the dog to perform this behavior without any external influence. This means that the focus shifts from the lure to the execution of the exercise as learning progresses.

Shaping, on the other hand, uses secondary reinforcers, such as a conditioned praise word or tools like a clicker. This guides the dog step by step toward the goal by immediately rewarding him for every progress made and thus conditioning him.

During this learning phase, constant reward is required.

Afterwards comes the phase called "flow". The desired behavior has already been learned fundamentally, so it's time for reinforcement. This is achieved by repeating the behavior frequently while applying signal control, which allows the dog to perform the behavior consciously and fluidly. Intermittent reinforcement is then used, which makes the training less predictable while motivation remains high due to occasional rewards. As for signal control, it means that the dog only performs the desired behavior upon a signal. Visual and auditory signals are differentiated, with an example being raising a finger or giving a clear command such as "sit" when the dog should do so. It makes sense to train both types of signals simultaneously to ensure equal reinforcement of both, allowing your dog to always listen to you, even if one of the signal types is unavailable - such as when you are sick and lose your voice or the dog becomes blind.

The third phase is called "Generalization". The signal control has been sufficiently repeated so that the dog follows it reliably. You continue your exercises but change the location of the training. If you have always trained in your own home, it's time for the garden, the forest, and later the city. The dog should learn to show the behavior at any time, not just in the familiar environment. This includes different places, times of day and night, varying environmental stimuli, and different situations.

The last phase is "Maintenance". Here, the learned behavior is frequently retrieved in any situation. This keeps the knowledge fresh and prevents it from being extinguished, which is why this phase lasts throughout the rest of the dog's life.

The types of learning:
This refers to whether you are applying classical or operant conditioning. It is important to be able to clearly distinguish between the two and adjust the exercises accordingly.

The learning techniques:
They are only relevant in the first phase, there is only luring or shaping. Which one is better suited can vary depending on the dog, situation, and exercise.

The goal and its respective criterion:
Ask yourself what you want to achieve and how this should happen. Remember to proceed as gradually as possible and not try to run before you can walk, or rather, before your dog can. Consider the progress your four-legged friend has already made and how creative he is in learning. The key is not to over- or under-challenge him.

The reward:
Make it dependent on the respective learning phase and situation. A tip: To improve the timing of the reward, you can ask another person to be present during training and observe you. They can give you tips on what could be improved.

In addition, there are many other questions that you can and should ask yourself before starting training, for example:

What is the best way to motivate my dog?

Do we both feel like learning right now?

Is my dog healthy or does he have physical complaints?

Is he rested enough?

How long can we both concentrate?

To make everything as clear as possible, you can create a training plan or diary in which you record the most important details, progress, and goals. This way, you always have an overview, even if life gets very stressful. The most important "rule": have fun doing it.

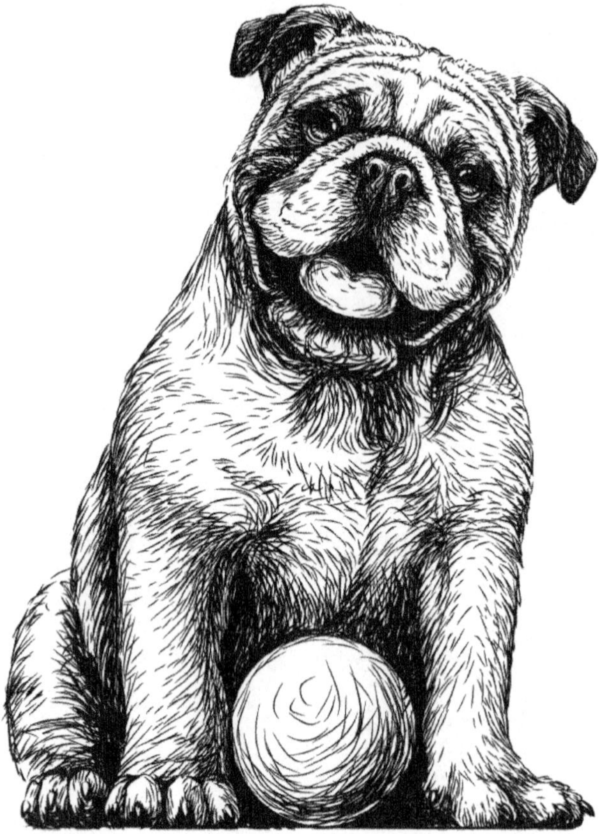

THE MOST COMMON EVERYDAY PROBLEMS WITH DOGS AND POSSIBLE SOLUTION STRATEGIES

In this final chapter, I would like to address the problems that are most widespread and have tested the patience of almost every dog owner. All of these behaviors can be trained and resolved wonderfully.

Successful leash training

Successfully walking on a leash is one of the first and most difficult challenges that new dog owners face. Once the dog is on the leash, he usually cannot stay calm. He pulls on the leash, sometimes so hard that it feels like he is taking the owner for a walk. If he is interested in something and wants to sniff while the owner wants to continue walking, he simply refuses to come along. In such situations, some people become desperate and pull on the leash until the dog is at risk of health problems. However, there are other ways to deal with this problem and ensure relaxed walks in the future (*Leash training for dogs - Are you leading or following?*, 2020).

In general, it can be said that the leash is not a tool for exerting pressure and should not be used to control the dog. It should not be used to convey emotions to the animal – especially not despair and powerlessness through frantic pulling. This would be counterproductive, as the dog constantly looks to you for guidance. He relies on you to have the situation under control and to safely guide him through the environment. You need to radiate this self-confidence. If you don't, the dog will take over the leadership and start pulling. Additionally, if the dog pulls, do not pull back! This is not a tug-of-war or a test of strength. It will not earn you any respect.

As for training, the rule is: the earlier you start, the better. Ideally, handling the leash should begin in puppyhood.

Now I would like to introduce you to some exercises that will bring you closer to solving this problem (*Train Loose Leash Walking: Tips and Tricks*, n.d.).

- Try relaxation. This is particularly important if you have felt insecure during previous walks and have been tempted to behave hectically. Whenever you notice that things could become stressful or your dog begins to pull, stand still without saying a word. Take deep breaths, gather yourself, and get an overview of the situation. Your dog will probably look at you strangely, then stop and wait to see what happens next. Communicate clearly through your body language that you need to re-establish your connection before proceeding. Don't stand around insecurely and stare into space. Even during such breaks, your dog must feel that you know what you are doing and he can follow you without reservation. You are always the leader he can trust. Then continue walking together. Observe how his behavior changes. Repeat this exercise as often as possible, as it also strengthens your relationship with each other.

- Make the walk exciting. To improve leash training, the dog must be focused on their owner and realize that they benefit more from exploring the area as a team instead of doing their own thing. To do this, you can provide additional stimuli by using hidden treats or their favorite toy that the dog can explore. Sounds such as the squeaking of a toy, calling their name, or attention-grabbing commands like "Look!" are also welcomed. Your dog will be more willing to follow you in the future if you don't just stick to your planned route.

- Counter stubbornness. This exercise is similar to the first one: when your dog exhibits unwanted behavior and pulls, stop walking. This time, it is not for your own calmness, but to set a clear signal. Just let your dog stand, even if the leash is under maximum tension. It is crucial that you do not pull back! Hold the leash firmly and signal to your dog that it is not going further, even if they strain. Ignore your dog at first and look in the direction in which you want to go next. Let them squirm a little, then call them to come to you. Once your dog looks at you consciously and waits for a command or even begins to continue in your chosen direction, they should be immediately and strongly rewarded. You do not necessarily have to stop, alternatively, you can turn around immediately and go in a different direction if your dog pulls. However, this assumes that your dog has accepted your authority to a sufficient extent and understands the signal and follows you. Otherwise, it could lead to a tug-of-war, which should be avoided.

Think specifically about the position your dog usually takes when walking and whether it is optimal. The typical "heel" position is not suitable for every dog, even if it looks impressive. Some dogs, especially fearful ones, need a certain distance and do not feel comfortable right next to their human. They prefer to walk a little behind, relying on their strong handler who has everything under control and paves the way for them by walking ahead. This makes them feel safer. It is concerning if a dog constantly walks in front of its owner. This is a clear indication that the dog is not comfortable with relinquishing responsibility - they simply don't trust the owner to be the leader. In this case, the owner must release the dog from this task and ensure that they take their place behind the human. It must be consistently shown that this is a role that the owner will not give up under any circumstances. The owner provides security, no one else.

If "heel" is desired and both parties are okay with it, there is not much to consider. Only one side should be established right at the beginning on which the dog will always be positioned to avoid future confusion.

Energetic barking when the doorbell rings

As soon as the doorbell rings, the dog starts barking and can hardly stop. It doesn't matter who is there. Whether it's the mail carrier or a friend, whether it's a persistent ringing or a quick press of the button. Does this sound familiar to you?

First, it's important to take a look at the possible causes. Dogs bark in this situation for a variety of reasons. Some are insecure or fearful and fear that there may be a danger behind the door. They want to drive it away with their barking. It may be that the dog has learned from an early age that the visit is intended for him, or he at least imagines it. If he walks to the door and is cuddled first due to his cuteness before the owner is greeted, the idea quickly arises that the dog should greet the visitor in the future. Whenever it rings now, an exciting play or cuddle session is most likely in store, which is why he expresses his anticipation with barking. Others show strong territorial behavior and want to defend their territory at all costs.

You can prevent it in the future by first identifying the cause and then selecting the appropriate strategy (*How to stop your dog from barking when the doorbell rings*, etc.):

- The dog who always greets visitors first must be taught to stay in his place and learn that his human always has priority. In the future, he should not be allowed to run freely to the door, but must remain in his place until you have opened the door and received the visitor. Take as much time as necessary, there is no reason to rush. If desired, the visitor can now enter, take off their shoes, and sit down. Then give the dog a release command to say hello. This exercise works best when the dog is accustomed to the "stay" command and does not see it as punishment to stay there. He should calm down and not sit on hot coals until he is allowed to leave his place. It is also helpful to work on habituation and get him used to the sound of the doorbell. Therefore, activate it occasionally without anyone wanting to see you. This can teach him that the doorbell is not necessarily associated with an exciting event.
- If the dog barks out of insecurity, the situation becomes more difficult. Here, a feeling of security must be established, but there is a reason why it is currently not present. This is often an indicator that something is wrong in your relationship with

your dog and he thinks he cannot trust you enough. For him, it seems as if you do not have the situation under control. It can help to "banish" the dog to his place when the bell rings. It is better if his place is not within sight of the door. On the one hand, he can then automatically relax more easily on his blanket, and on the other hand, he will gradually realize that you do not need his presence to handle the situation. This way, you can convey the leader status again and relieve him of his stressful task. However, it may be that fear and insecurity are so deeply ingrained that you cannot make any progress. In this case, it is useful, as with too strong territorial behavior, to seek the help of a behavioral therapist for dogs.

The wrong greeting for visitors

Excited barking is unfavorable when greeting people. It is even worse when the dog jumps on people without warning. This not only soils clothing but can also cause fear, which is why this behavior should be trained out as soon as possible.

There are various reasons why dogs jump up on people. On the one hand, it can be due to excitement and the desire for attention, while on the other hand, it can be a way to establish the hierarchy within an imaginary pack. In most cases, it is a learned behavior that was solidified in puppyhood. Somewhere, it is understandable: when a little, cute puppy approaches you and stands up, you feel the need to squat down and cuddle him. He learns that it is okay and even rewarded to greet people in this way. This is precisely what will later cause problems when he is bigger.

What you can do (*Does your dog jump up on you and other people?*):

- Stop this behavior physically. This means that you or the other person prevent the dog from jumping up in the first place. Hold onto his front paws and set him down. Alternatively, the leash can be shortened. What is important here is to use only simple body signals. The dog must not be looked at or addressed. The statement would be irrelevant here – he would get the attention he desires.
- Ignoring, turning away or walking away are other options. This must be consistently carried out by everyone it affects.
- It can also be effective to demonstrate alternative behavior and reinforce it. If your dog, for example, knows "down" very well, he should lie down calmly before the other person comes. When people have greeted each other, the dog can be petted.

Furthermore, if possible, you should inform other people before they come to you. Clearly and clearly tell them that your dog tends to jump up and what you expect from the person. Unfortunately, there are people who do not take the dog owner's requests seriously or ignore them on principle, thereby encouraging the dog's misbehavior. If you know someone like this, you should try to avoid meeting them in the future when the dog is present.

Problems with feeding

Problems can arise when feeding a dog in the form of begging or aggressive behavior. Rarely are these behaviors inherent in the nature of the dog; in most cases, the owner has caused them (*The most common mistakes in dog feeding*, 2022).

Often, the owner means well when observing their dog while eating. They want to ensure that their dog eats everything and is full. Sometimes, in the midst of a busy day, they may want to give their dog a little snack to make them happy. What is particularly dangerous is that some people want to demonstrate their dominance and power by regularly taking away their dog's bowl while they eat and forcing them to accept it. If the dog does not comply, they are threatened with punishment. Let's take a look at what these points can do in the dog's mind: if they can never eat in peace, they may try to eat their food as quickly as possible. They want to eat as much as possible because they are afraid that their food will soon be taken away and they may not get any more. Perhaps they are afraid to approach their full bowl, as they conclude from their higher-ranking owner's behavior that they claim the meal for themselves. In the worst case, they may even defend their food. This is done through threatening gestures, growling, and snapping if necessary. This behavior is particularly noticeable towards children, as they are considered equal members of the pack, and the dog wants to signal to them that this is their prey that they claim for themselves. Especially with small children who are very curious and cannot interpret the dog's warnings, this can create a very dangerous situation.

How can you address this issue? You should ensure that your dog can eat in peace and without any disturbance at all times. The best way to do this is in a separate room where he is not disturbed or observed by anyone - neither by you nor by another pet. If you have to take the filled bowl away in between, send the dog to another room first. Don't just interfere while he is eating. Show him that you respect when he eats.

Let's move on to the issue of begging. This is caused by the fact that we sometimes want to give our dog an extra treat, for example, when he has been patiently waiting for our return all day, or when we feel guilty for indulging ourselves with a snack or a particularly fine meal. Or, when he wants attention at an inappropriate moment and won't leave the owner alone, a treat is an easy way to temporarily quiet the pushy dog. However, what this triggers in the dog should not be underestimated: eventually, food is seen as a substitute for love and attention. Additionally, the more treats he gets, the more likely he is to become overweight and his regular meal is no longer attractive. He also internalizes the behavior he needs to show to get food and thus begs more and more frequently. The desire for play or cuddles decreases until the owner eventually becomes nothing more than a human food dispenser. Regardless of how you look at it, giving your dog treats for no reason does him no favors. This can have serious consequences for the relationship and bond you have with your dog.

The question comes up: How can you address the issue if you have already made this mistake several times and your dog regularly begs?

- Give him a lot of attention that you express in other ways. Play with him, cuddle together, brush him. Don't express your love through food, but show him that he is so important to you that you want to spend regular and extensive time with him.
- If you have mainly used treats as rewards during training, you should prefer other means.
- You can still use food as an activity if you really don't have time. Instead of just giving it to him, you should use a food toy. This keeps him busy in the long term, he eats less and slower, and he learns in passing that he has to work for his food.

A tip: Since some treats are used during an intensive training session, you should subtract this food from his main meal. This way, he won't consume any extra calories and obesity will be prevented.

Learning to be alone

Dogs are highly social pack animals, and it is in their nature to feel particularly comfortable when other dogs or humans are present. Therefore, it is more difficult for them to have to be alone for long periods of time. On the one hand, there is the fear of being left behind, and on the other hand, without their caregiver, they often experience a loss of control that overwhelms them (*Leaving your dog alone & avoiding separation anxiety*, n.d.).

There is no clear answer to the question of how long one can leave their dog alone. It depends on the condition and type of dog. Some may even fall into depressive states because of it. The time should not exceed five hours if possible. By then, the dog will urgently need to take care of its business. If the dog has access to a large yard, for example, this may not be a problem. In an apartment, however, the fear of punishment can creep in if the dog is forced to go to the bathroom in the apartment, even though it has learned differently.

We have already established how important it is for the human to take on the role of the alpha and fully fulfill it. He is the great protector who sets the direction. Conversely, this circumstance poses the risk that the dog is completely at a loss whenever his alpha is absent. Especially if he has experienced intense separation anxiety before, the condition worsens with each occurrence and the dog begins to cling to you. Such separation anxiety can be triggered by three different factors. For example, it is observed in animals that were separated from their mother and siblings too early in their puppyhood. The first bonds are built with them. If this process is disrupted, the dog cannot develop a healthy basic trust. Animals that have spent a longer period in the animal shelter and were subsequently rehomed have often suffered traumas and developed fears due to the loss of their previous owner. Last but not least, it is also possible that they are caused by educational mistakes. If the human treats every short-term separation like a final farewell, strokes the dog excessively long, and tries to console him, then the dog concludes that something bad is about to happen. This is not a good foundation for anxious dogs.

You recognize urgent need for action based on the following behaviors:

- If a dog suffers from separation anxiety, he becomes sad as soon as the door closes behind you. He may remain there for hours waiting for your return, and he may scratch doors and walls or start to howl. It may even lead to him relieving himself, not because he urgently needs to, but as a side effect of panic. Based on the greeting, you'll notice that something is wrong: If it's exuberant but the dog remains submissive and immediately submits, it indicates a strong dependence on the alpha leader that he misses so much.
- On the other hand, loss of control is expressed in aggressive behavior, which often targets furniture, pillows, and other objects in your home inventory. He can express his frustration, much to the delight of the neighbors, through loud and prolonged barking. Pay attention to the greeting: If he jumps on you wildly, it's not necessarily a sign of joy, but rather a punishment for leaving him alone.

While separation anxiety evokes sadness, with control loss it is anger. Like all controlling dogs, he sees it as his task to protect you – if you intentionally go out into the dangerous world without him, he worries about you and is upset that he can't fulfill this task. In this case, the approach is similar: show the dog that you can take care of yourself and take on this role. You achieve this by leaving the house quite naturally, as if it were the most normal thing in the world. No farewell, nothing at all. You come back shortly afterwards. Extend the time period continuously until he eventually learns that nothing happens to you and he can relax.

You can use the following exercise to address the fear: Lead your dog to his place and provide him with something to occupy himself, such as a chew bone or a toy. Once he's focused on that and not paying attention to you, quietly leave the room. Then wait for your dog's reaction: Does he start whining or does he remain quiet for the moment? Wait for a brief period, then return to your dog once he has definitively calmed down. Reward him lavishly for waiting patiently. Over time, you can extend the duration of your absence. At first, you may just go to the next room, eventually leave the house/apartment, and later stay away for longer periods. Use the time to go shopping or meet someone for coffee in peace. Eventually, your dog will internalize that you always come back to him and will become less fearful.

Aggressiveness towards other dogs

It becomes particularly tricky when the dog simply cannot get along with its own kind. Whenever he encounters other dogs, he pulls heavily on the leash. He would like to break free, bares his teeth, growls and hardly listens. It's as if a switch has been flipped in his head, sending him from zero to a hundred and immediately seeing red. It doesn't matter what intentions the other animal has, whether it even notices him or whether it is three times his size. As an owner, one quickly becomes nervous because you cannot go for a walk without fearing a dangerous escalation.

To get closer to a solution, it is important that you become aware of the following: Dogs that exhibit this behavior are usually very temperamental. You cannot change this character trait, no matter how much you wish to. Please do not think you have to fight against your dog. Instead, you are the rock in the surf that shows him how to handle his anger and excitement properly and redirect these feelings so that it does not lead to baseless aggression.

Aggressive dogs are by no means inherently hostile or evil – they are simply overwhelmed and see aggression as a last resort because they do not know how to handle the situation. They do not want to act this way. They need our help, we need to take them by the hand. This requires authority, calmness, and understanding. Punishments such as scolding, jerking the leash abruptly, or desperately listing commands in the hope that something will help are completely out of place here and would only further exacerbate the dog's frustration.

Let's get to the root cause of this problem. As so often, it is fear combined with uncertainty. This is based on the feeling of not being able to solve the encounter with other dogs in the group. He feels abandoned by the owner in the situation, since he approaches the situation incorrectly. Instead of just letting the encounter happen and remaining relaxed, he worries and thinks about what could happen. Is the other dog friendly? Will he growl at his dog? Does he want to play? Will he suddenly bite at worst? The dog notices these fears. On the one hand, the owner could act by, for example, taking his dog on a shorter leash and pulling him closer to his body just before the encounter. This automatically signals "attention, something is about to happen". On the other hand, these worries are reflected in his posture, facial expression and gestures. This makes the dog think "damn, my human is afraid of the other dog and can't handle this situation alone. Therefore, I'll take over and show the other dog that he should leave us alone!" This can go so far that he not only reacts like this in encounters, but wants to attack dogs in general as soon as they appear in his field of vision. All in line with the theme: "I'll attack first before you do anything to me/us". Therefore, his aggressiveness is an exercise in group dynamics, as he wants to protect his pack and his human signals that he needs protection. Accordingly, educational measures in this situation are unlikely to be successful, as the owner would be fighting against his instincts that are not in his genes for nothing.

I cannot give you an exercise for this, as this problem cannot be solved through training. Technically speaking, it is not a behavior that can be unlearned, so neither rewards nor punishments will do anything. It should not be considered to attempt a confrontation therapy by forcefully bringing the dogs together. Since he would have no way back, it becomes even more dangerous if the stress becomes too great. In this case, it happens very quickly. To find an effective solution here, you should primarily work on yourself. Think about why you are skeptical about encounters with strange dogs. Have you had bad experiences before? Do you not trust the other owner because you see that he does not have his dog under control? Has your dog been bitten by another dog in the past and you are afraid it could happen again? Are you generally an anxious person? Check if you can work on yourself in this regard and regularly control yourself. It may be that you have to work through something that you have previously suppressed. Be open to improving yourself. If you radiate strength, calmness, and security, you will notice how the dog's behavior changes dramatically. The aggression will not stop immediately, but if you keep proving that you do not need protection and that the other dog is not a threat, your dog will notice and adapt accordingly. This will be an immense relief for the dog, as he fundamentally feels a high need for peace and harmony. He does not want senseless stress with other dogs, and physical confrontations certainly not. Whether one believes it or not: this applies to every single dog (Hebel, n.d.), all deviations are due to the influence of the owner.

By the way, whenever you notice that the situation could become dangerous, for example, because the other dog seems agitated and aggressive, do not put yourself in that situation. Make the decision promptly and turn into another street, change direction or something similar before the encounter. Act as if it were the most normal thing in the world. You should not panic or flee. You are in control and decide that you will go somewhere else today. Period.

When your dog chases after cars or bicycles.

Does your dog enjoy chasing everything that moves quickly past him? This behavior can be dangerous, both for the cyclist and for the four-legged friend, who often races recklessly into the street in his frenzy.

The reasoning behind such behavior is obvious: the dog's hunting instinct is far from satisfied, so he seeks alternatives. This disposition is present in every dog, but few are actually involved in hunting or have other ways to satisfy this urge. The highest point of excitement may be when the hated neighbor's cat is lurking on your property. Speaking of property: there are dogs that act like this due to their territorial behavior - they want to chase away the "intruder" as quickly as possible and usually stop as soon as he has finally left their area. As this is a sensitive issue that cannot be easily resolved by laypeople, I refer to a dog trainer here. As for the unfulfilled hunting needs, there are several things you can do. During training, exercises or tools that address this need should be used as often as possible. Since hunting involves many different aspects, you need to find out which of these tasks your dog would enjoy taking on. Retrieving, chasing, reading tracks, or searching for "prey" such as food, toys, and the like - all of these things are great fun for dogs and easy to implement. In the case of a dog that chases after things, chasing will be the focus. This is not the same as classic running, as it would be enough to throw a ball quickly with another person and let the dog run. However, there is still a great way to do this, namely the so-called teaser stick. You can build such a stick yourself by taking a sturdy stick and attaching a long, robust cord to it. The "prey" for your dog is fixed at the other end of the cord. This can be food, a toy, or something completely different. It is important that the object is not too heavy and can be easily moved. Get your furry friend's attention on the prey and throw it a short distance away. When the dog runs, move the prey a little further using the stick. At first, it should not be too wild and the dog should succeed relatively easily. Over time, you can let him chase longer and faster. Spontaneous changes of direction make it more exciting.

This exercise can be ideally complemented with impulse control training, which is designed to help the dog resist the tempting lure of the toy and the moving prey. Use the insights from the first chapter for this purpose. In addition, habituation should be aimed for, where the dog ultimately learns not to react to passing cars or cyclists. Therefore, move your training to a suitable environment, such as a park with bike paths or near a road. For safety, the dog should remain on a leash during the training (Theobald-Hoffmann, 2021).

The dog is missing and the recall doesn't work

Just a moment ago, you were walking relaxedly on a country lane, when suddenly your four-legged friend runs off without warning, leaving you behind. You call him as often and as loudly as you can, but every recall is ignored. You wait for a few minutes, but the dog doesn't seem to be coming back. Negative thoughts quickly arise: Has something happened to him? Does he need help? Where could he be now? If you have to leave at some point, will he find his way home or wander around lost? How do you find him? The worries are great, the perplexity even greater.

To avoid such a situation, there is a way to get your dog to listen to your recall command. First, you need to understand that recall is a complex behavior. It's not as easy to train as you might think. After all, your dog didn't just run away for no reason: there is a specific stimulus that he wants to follow at all costs. The recall command means that he has to be clear in his thinking to understand the command and then immediately obey it, which he may not like if it means giving up the exciting stimulus. From there, he has to come back to you on the most direct path, resisting all other distractions he encounters along the way. As you can see, this requires a lot of effort from the dog, which is not something he will do naturally. Remember that dogs are selfish and do things for a specific motivation. This means that you need to offer him something that is more rewarding than his exploration. Otherwise, he will not voluntarily come back to you, or he will do so only after he has thoroughly satisfied his desire, which can take a while. Therefore, it can be concluded that it is not useful to scold him when he returns. On the contrary, if he runs away again, he will return later to avoid the punishment.

In general, if your dog has ever gone missing, you should consider getting a long leash if you haven't already done so. This makes training easier and prevents a repeat of this situation if the recall fails again. Furthermore, it must be considered how dangerous it can be when the dog runs around uncontrolled. Not only for him, but also for the environment and other animals. However, the long leash should not be used for training and is only the last resort before losing control of the dog. It is not used to pull the dog back to you if he refuses to listen, as this prevents the desire to want to come back to you voluntarily.

Here are some tips and exercises that I can offer you:

- If your dog goes missing, keep trying to call them back. Stay where they left you, and don't run after them or away from them. It can be exhausting to call them repeatedly, but it's the only logical behavior that has a training aspect to it. You may need to try calling them 50 times if necessary. You have to train with them anyway, so use this unfavorable situation as a training opportunity. Even though this situation is anything but pleasant, try to keep a cool head. Don't lose your nerves and panic, as it won't help. Once your dog comes back to you, leash them again and reward them abundantly for returning to you. This will show them that there is something in it for them if they come to you.

- It's possible that your dog may come closer to you and stay at an acceptable distance, but not close enough to leash. This often happens out of spite or a dislike for the leash. At this point, you may be emotionally drained. Take a deep breath, gather your strength, and calmly walk over to your dog to leash them. Pay attention to your body language! If you approach them angrily and stormily with the leash in your hand, your dog may perceive this behavior as threatening, which may reduce their desire to be leashed. Once they are secured, reward them nonetheless. This will show them that there is no other way and that it's not that bad.

- In a calm moment, reflect on this situation. What was the lure that captivated your dog and caused them to run away? Identify this strong distraction. Then consider how to avoid it in the future. Does it make sense to choose a different route for walks, at least temporarily? Or is it sufficient to be more attentive next time to recognize potential distractions early and intervene? Should your dog never be off-leash again? Additionally, think about whether there is anything you could add or improve in training to help your dog better cope with distractions (Seumel, 2020).

When hands suddenly become a target

Many dog owners are lenient, especially with puppies. After all, it's hard to be mad at them, right? So it's also accepted when the little one starts nibbling on the hands of humans while being petted or during other occasions. Somehow it's cute and with their little teeth it doesn't hurt much. Additionally, the dog doesn't do this with malicious intent, but out of affection. If this aspect is not taken seriously and this behavior is encouraged by playing along, it will eventually lead to an unpleasant situation. This can look different, maybe he underestimates his strength and bites seriously, maybe he pinches a child too hard, which then gets scared, screams and develops a fear of the dog. Either way, it's not acceptable and further steps must be taken to stop this behavior.

Let's first take a look at why young dogs especially like to bite their owners' hands: It is an indirect compliment, as the dog sees the human as a member of their pack and wants to show their appreciation. After all, they can't use their paws to pat them back. In addition, teeth are used to establish the hierarchy among pack members, to calm each other down, or to groom the fur. If you are faced with this problem, please keep in mind that this behavior does not automatically mean that your dog could become aggressive or seriously injure you later in life (*Why is the dog nibbling on me?*, 2022).

There are several ways to solve this problem:

When dealing with puppies and young dogs, it makes sense to apply the muzzle grab and neck tap. What may sound extreme at first is actually normal behavior that mother animals use to show their young boundaries. The neck tap can also be observed when adult dogs play with each other. In general, it is important to start this training as early as possible and not wait until the situation escalates. Establish a word that immediately stops the dog's behavior. "No" is not the best option, as humans use this word so frequently in everyday life that the dog may not take it seriously and never know when it is being addressed. You can say "Taboo," "Enough," or something similar. Here's how to proceed (Sporrer, 2022a):

Use a toy that your dog likes to chew on to protect your hands and place it in front of him. He will try to reach it, but you do not want him to. Meet him with a stern look, be prepared that he will not take it seriously. If the dog continues, briefly hold onto the snout and use your interrupt word to condition it. Depending on how often he has experienced the snout grip from his mother, he may squeak in fright. This does not mean you have hurt him! Of course, you should not cause him pain, but the pressure should be noticeable so that he takes this discipline seriously. It may be that the dog's snout is not reachable for you at times. In this case, resort to the neck bump: Mimic a snout with your hand and give the dog a little nudge in the neck area. However, it must be a nudge, not a push, as this could further animate him. The word is also used simultaneously here.

What to keep in mind with these two tactics: timing is everything. If several seconds have already passed since the dog showed the unwanted chewing behavior, they lose their effectiveness. You may be wondering at this point how useful the application is, as it sounds like punishment. That is not the case! As long as you do not use violence, the dog will see this as normal behavior among peers and you do not have to worry about your relationship suffering. Do not be tempted to "apologize" to him afterwards or distract him because you feel guilty. Leave the dog alone and ignore him so he can learn from the situation. If he comes back after a few minutes and seeks your proximity, allow this. However, show him that he still cannot go for his chew toy, your hands, or other objects, no matter how appeasing he may appear.

Let's move on to adult dogs that like to bite hands. Here, the snout grip and neck shove can be difficult because the dog has already learned that it can get away with small acts of disrespect and you have not clearly set some boundaries. If you want to put yourself in the superior role of the mother animal or an equal pack member, your dog may not take you seriously by principle. In this case, it becomes necessary to rely on conditioning and work with reinforcements. Working with treats or other rewards can be difficult here, but try it anyway. Otherwise, if necessary, work through deliberately applied ignorance or pulling away your hands, after which you leave and leave the dog sitting. Don't respond to the biting and show him that there are other ways to express his affection. As for a pronounced chewing need, you can offer him a chew toy, a chew stick, or something similar, which he can chew on as he pleases. As long as you clearly define that he only chews on it, you have created a good distraction and the dog does not have to do without anything.

The dog doesn't voluntarily give up its bone or toy

Having to take something away from your dog that they are currently engaged with should not be a regular occurrence, but it may become necessary under certain circumstances. If the dog reacts with bared teeth, growling, or aggressive behavior, the alarm bells should be ringing in your head. This signals that the object is a resource of great importance to the dog and that it does not want to give it up. This can be any number of things, as each dog has individual preferences. It has been observed that dogs exhibit this behavior towards babies. They stand over or behind the unsuspecting child, growling and trying to prevent the parents from getting too close. While this may initially seem like a lovable protective instinct, in reality it is quite the opposite, as the dog views the baby as prey. This situation is very dangerous for everyone involved and can quickly escalate, so it is important to teach the dog to relinquish their claimed resources on command.

These are the options available to you when looking for a solution:

- Trade with the dog. This exercise is the easiest as the dog doesn't have to give up anything, in fact, he gets something better. This can be a favorite toy or something similar that you know he prefers. On the other hand, a new item that he has not seen before and that piques his interest can also work. Present this exchange offer to him. If he takes the new thing, take away the old resource. Over time, he will be conditioned to expect something good when you approach him to claim the item. In the future, interesting trade items should always be provided.
- As part of further training, it makes sense to reinforce the "drop it" command, where the dog immediately drops whatever he has in his mouth. Since this signal has been trained through positive reinforcement, the dog will usually be happy to comply as he looks forward to the impending reward.
- With food, things become a bit more delicate as dogs usually defend it more energetically than other resources. After all, food is more important for survival than a ball. Here, it is advisable to offer "better" food as an alternative. As we have already seen, there are different gradations since dogs do not treat every food equally. Dry food that is perhaps given every day has a completely different value than the great liver sausage from the tube that he has earned through special efforts. You should always be able to trump the food your dog is currently defending. Since this will be the classic bowl or a chew bone, it should not be too difficult. Proceed in the same way as with any other trade.

In conclusion: Never take away your dog's resources just because it's fun for you or because you want to exert power. This is a group dynamic behavior that signals to other pack members to stay away from that item and that the particular dog has claimed it. This is accepted and respected unless there is an exceptional situation, such as when food is scarce and the alpha dog claims the ration.

Consequently, it is not common or even seen as an attack when another animal comes and simply takes the resource away. It is already difficult for the dog to accept this from you, so there should always be something positive for him to maintain a good relationship with you. Show the necessary respect and only intervene when absolutely necessary (*Der Hund gibt Spielzeug/Knochen nicht ab!*, 2019).

When the whole garden is dug up

Let's turn to the last everyday problem: what to do when your dog digs up the beloved garden in your absence, leaving a trail of destruction?

There are several reasons why dogs behave like this. One reason could be a strong hunting instinct, as small creatures can be found in every garden that pique their interest. These include, for example, mice or moles. Dogs pick up the smells of these animals with their sensitive noses. If simply sniffing the earth or the entrance to the burrow is not enough, they will dig up the soil to get closer. Digging can be used by resourceful dogs, especially those that are in heat or pregnant, to create a protected nesting area in the earth. The resulting holes could also be used to store a small supply of leftover treats for later enjoyment. Additionally, you could be the trigger for this behavior: if you enjoy working in the garden and do so regularly, the dog will watch you with interest. At some point, the urge to try it out themselves takes over. Especially when you have previously dug up the earth and made it nice and loose, it is an invitation to dig. Let's move on to the probably most common reason: boredom. If the dog lacks stimulation or is alone for too long, it will look for something to occupy itself. Since there is not much for them to do in the garden, they will soon become interested in the soil. Additionally, their digging is always rewarded with the attention they crave from you, even if you express your disappointment or anger with a disappointed sigh.

Let's talk about what you can do about it (Melchior, 2021):

- Before your extended absence, make sure all of your dog's needs are met. Was he well-exercised? Does he have a comfortable resting area? If he's a hunting dog, is his hunting drive sufficiently satisfied?
- If you spend a lot of time working in the garden, you should avoid allowing your dog to view gardening as one of his tasks and want to help you. You can bring his blanket from the blanket exercise into the garden and have him lie down there while you pursue your hobby. If this doesn't work, you can leash him at some distance. Avoid having him stand next to you and control every movement.
- Alternatively, you can involve your dog in the work. But, this should happen in a controlled and environment determined by you. If you're okay with it, you can assign your dog his own area where he can dig as much as he wants, provided he leaves the rest of the garden alone. This area should be large enough and refilled regularly so that he doesn't lose interest. You can hide treats there to encourage digging at first. Whenever he starts digging in another spot, lead him to that area. However, it should be noted that this approach may not work and you are taking a certain risk.
- Stop any digging with learned tactics, preferably using commands such as "No," "Stop," "Taboo," or similar.
- If nothing works or you have to wait a long time for results, you should focus on protecting your garden beds. Instead of having to be afraid every day, take precautions with fences or similar enclosures. Raised beds can be a nice alternative that not only protects your harvest but also looks great. Of course, this doesn't prevent digging, but it might be less annoying if the

dog only digs under the hedge and doesn't pull your carefully grown carrots out of the ground.

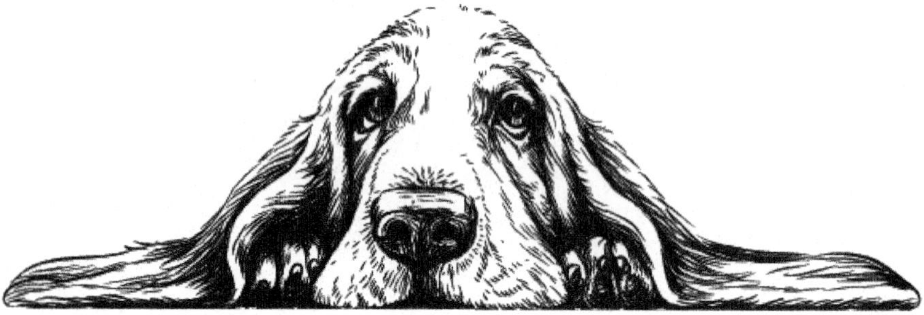

CLOSING WORDS

You have now learned all the important basics you need for dog training. You can put aside the fear that finding the right method is like looking for a needle in a haystack. Say goodbye to countless guides, all-knowing experts, and the abundance of conflicting opinions. It's time for you to use your knowledge to create your own method. With the necessary patience, joy, and great understanding, you will find the path that is perfect for your dog and you. Of course, it may happen that you see other owners with their four-legged friends and feel the need to imitate them. After all, it works so well for them, so it would certainly be sensible to try it that way. If you keep the psychological basics in mind and approach the matter wisely, this may be true. Please never forget that every dog has unique needs and other problems that need to be solved. You cannot compare a perfectly healthy young dog with an older dog who may not see as well and may also suffer from a chronic illness. In addition, one should never forget that one often does not know what history the animal has already gone through. A dog from a reliable breeder who then goes to a loving home is a completely different case than one who has already been abused multiple times and has had to survive alone on the street for some time. Every four-legged friend has different requirements and needs that need to be fulfilled. Let go of expectations and accept your dog as he is – with all his quirks and imperfections. With the right approach, you will always be able to teach him what he needs to learn. Regardless of the starting point, you can and will achieve your goal. Let go of fixed schemas and go on an exploration tour. Get to know each other properly and love each other so that you can enjoy life together to the fullest. I wish you much success on your continued journey, believe in yourself!

Free-Bonus:

92 DOG EXERCISES with brain teasers and intelligence exercises.

Scan the QR code with your phone camera and go directly to the bonus download.

SOURCE INFORMATION:

Blaschke-Berthold. (2020, 23. Mai). Die konditionierte Entspannung beim Hund - Aufbau, Anwendung im Alltag und Fehlerquellen im Training. Easy Dogs. Abgerufen am 8. August 2022, von https://www.easy-dogs.net/konditionierte-entspannung/

Colino, S. (2021, 5. Oktober). Eine ganze Reihe neuer Studien belegt, dass Hunde die Gefühle von Menschen nicht nur wahrnehmen können, sondern sich diese auch auf sie übertragen. National Geographic. Abgerufen am 12. August 2022, von https://www.nationalgeographic.de/tiere/2021/10/ansteckende-emotionen-hundeund-ihre-besitzer-fuehlen-gleich

Deckentraining - so kann Dein Hund überall entspannen. (2022, 9. Februar). Floxik Premium Hundeprodukte. Abgerufen am 8. August 2022, von https://www.floxik.de/deckentraining/

Doguniversity [Doguniversity - Hundetraining mit Daniel]. (2020, 1. November). So testest Du die Bindung zwischen dir und deinem Hund [Video]. YouTube.
https://www.youtube.com/watch?v=F81m4mxhKnI

Entspannter Spaziergang mit Hund – Teil 1: Trödeln. (2018, 4. März). Bothshunde. Abgerufen am 11. August 2022, von https://bothshunde.com/entspannter-spaziergang-mithund-teil-1-troedeln/#:%7E:text=Ein%20weitl%C3%A4ufiger%20Waldweg%20oder%20eine,lieber%20an%20einer%20langen%20Leine.

Frustrationstoleranz beim Hund – Übungen zum Nachmachen. (2022, 14. Mai). Floxik Premium Hundeprodukte. Abgerufen am 2. August 2022, von https://www.floxik.de/frustrationstoleranz-beim-hund/

Die häufigsten Fehler bei der Hundefütterung. (2022, 10. Februar). Tierarzt Dr. Hölter. Abgerufen am 14. August 2022, von https://www.drhoelter.de/tierarzt/ernaehrungsinfos/die-haeufigsten-fehler-bei-der-hundefuetterung.html?fbclid=IwAR1TB25rOV7dnhVzWdKj01hSCGz61q A4xf2ZiFSCv_mA7LCefosLLGQaYwQ

Hebel, A. (o. D.). Hunde-Aggression zu Artgenossen erfolgreich beenden. Cityhunde.de. Abgerufen am 15. August 2022, von https://www.cityhunde.de/blog/blog-hundeverhalten/25-hunde-aggression-zu-artgenossen-beenden?fbclid=IwAR0sOlbUoBf75cQUYu1X11sCWXVM_F2ofeJ fN-wMalYIhR79JuREROCWVRk

Hund alleine lassen & Trennungsangst vermeiden. (o. D.). FRESSNAPF. Abgerufen am 15. August 2022, von https://www.fressnapf.at/magazin/hund/erziehung/alleine-lassen/?fbclid=IwAR2kT_Ey3d4gNj9ib1fiKswE9i_CgyXGXLc0XQQ2OT RBe geHK2o9_wMu6v4

Der Hund gibt Spielzeug/Knochen nicht ab! (2019, 23. Juni). Rhein-Neckar Dogs. Abgerufen am 16. August 2022, von https://www.rhein-neckar-dogs.de/post/mein-hundgibt-spielzeug-knochen-nicht-mehr-her

Hund Sozialisierung und Prägung. (o. D.). Mera Petfood. Abgerufen am 7. August 2022, von https://www.mera-petfood.com/de/hund/ratgeber/welpen-wissen-welpenwelt/hund-sozialisierung/#:%7E:text=durch%20andere%20Hunde,Die%20Pr%C3%A4gung%20des%20Welpen,m%C3%B6glich%20kennenlernen%20und%20positiv%20abspeichern.

Impulskontrolle bei Hunden - kostenlose Übungen. (2022, 28. April). Hundeschulkonzepte. Abgerufen am 1. August 2022, von https://hundeschulkonzepte.de/ubungen-zur-impulskontrolle-bei-hunden/ Impulskontrolle beim Hund. (2022, 9. Februar). Petplan DE. Abgerufen am 20. Juli 2022, von https://petplan.de/impulskontrolle-beimhund/#:%7E:text=Impulskontrolle%20bedeutet%2C%20%20dass%20Ihr%20Hund,und%20zu%20Ihn en%20zu%20kommen

Leinenführigkeit trainieren: Infos & Tipps. (o. D.). FRESSNAPF. Abgerufen am 14. August 2022, von https://www.fressnapf.de/magazin/hund/erziehung/leinenfuehrigkeit/#leinenf%C3%BChrigkeit

Leinenführung beim Hund – Führst du schon oder folgst du noch? (2020, 9. Juni). Lernpfote. Abgerufen am 13. August 2022, von https://lernpfote.de/blog/leinenfuehrung-beimhund/

Lerntheorie: im Hundetraining richtig eingesetzt - Teil 5/5. (2016, 2. März). Hundeherz.ch. Abgerufen am 12. August 2022, von https://www.hundeherz.ch/fachbeitrag/lerntheoriehund-im-hundetraining-richtig-eingesetzt-teil-5

Lerntheorie: Positiv belohnen, gewusst wie – Teil 4/5. (2016, 2. März). Hundeherz.ch. Abgerufen am 12. August 2022, von https://www.hundeherz.ch/fachbeitrag/lerntheoriehund-positiv-belohnen-gewusst-wie-teil-4

Lerntheorie: Positive und negative Verstärker – Teil 3/5. (2016, 2. März). Hundeherz.ch. Abgerufen am 12. August 2022, von https://www.hundeherz.ch/fachbeitrag/lerntheoriehund-positive-und-negative-verstaerker-teil-3

Lerntheorie: Wichtigste Lernprozesse – Teil 2/5. (2015, 27. November). Hundeherz.ch. Abgerufen am 13. August 2022, von https://www.hundeherz.ch/fachbeitrag/lerntheoriehund-wichtigste-lernprozesse-teil-2

Lerntheorie: Wie lernt ein Hund – Teil 1/5. (2017, 3. April). Hundeherz.ch. Abgerufen am 12. August 2022, von https://www.hundeherz.ch/fachbeitrag/lerntheorie-wielernt-ein-hund-teil-1

Melchior, L. (2021, 28. April). Warum buddelt mein Hund im Garten? zooplus Magazine. Abgerufen am 24. August 2022, von https://www.zooplus.de/magazin/hund/hundeerziehung/warum-buddelt-mein-hund-im-garten

Nubi, M. V. H. (2022, 2. Januar). 3 Übungen zur Impulskontrolle für deinen Hund. Hundesport Nubi. Abgerufen am 1. August 2022, von https://hundesport-nubi.de/impulskontrolleueben-mit-hund/

Oberli, T.-M. (2022, 31. Mai). Die Hundezunge. TeamSchule für Mensch und Hund. Abgerufen am 10. August 2022, von https://teamschule.blog/2022/05/29/die-hundezunge/

Quast, K. (2021, 28. Januar). Frustrationstoleranz beim Hund aufbauen. VOLLZEIT4BEINER. Abgerufen am 3. August 2022, von https://vollzeit4beiner.at/frustrationstoleranz-beim-hund Seumel, U. (2020, 18. Februar). Was tun, wenn der Rückruf nicht klappt. Dog It Right | Blog. Abgerufen am 15. August 2022, von https://blog.dogitright.de/rueckruf-nicht-klappt/

A shoulder to cry on: Heart rate variability and empathetic behavioral responses to crying and laughing in dogs. (o. D.). Pubmed. Abgerufen am 12. August 2022, von https://pubmed.ncbi.nlm.nih.gov/33090854/

Sporrer, C. (2022a, Mai 30). „Hilfe, mein Hund beißt in meine Hände!" 2022 Martin Rütter DOGS, Conny Sporrer. Abgerufen am 23. August 2022, von https://www.martinruetter.com/wien/news/details/artikel/hilfe-mein-hundbeisst-in-meine-haende/#:%7E:text=Daf%C3%BCr%20gibt%20es%20zumeist%20zwei,die%20Ma%C3%9Fregelung%20sinnvoll%20zu%20setzen. Sporrer, C. (2022b, Mai 30). IMPULSKONTROLLE. 2022 Martin Rütter DOGS, Conny Sporrer. Abgerufen am 1. August 2022, von https://www.martinruetter.com/wien/news/details/artikel/impulskontrolle-1/

Springt dein Hund an dir und anderen Menschen hoch? (o. D.). MyLuckyDog. Abgerufen am 13. August 2022, von https://myluckydog.ch/blog/springt-dein-hund-an-dirund-anderen-menschen-hoch

Theobald-Hoffmann, R. (2021, 19. September). DOGS Tipp Oktober: Unerwünschtes Jagdverhalten: Wenn Hunde Autos jagen . . . 2022 Martin Rütter DOGS, Richarda TheobaldHoffmann. Abgerufen am 15. August 2022, von https://www.martinruetter.com/stwendelkaiserslautern/trainingstipps/dogs-trainingstipp/artikel/dogstipp-oktober-unerwuenschtes-jagdverhalten-wennhunde-autos-jagen/

Ursachen & Gründe für einen unruhigen oder gestressten Hund [Teil 3]. (2022, 3. Februar). Vitomalia. Abgerufen am 5. August 2022, von https://vitomalia.com/blogs/news/hundegesundheit-ursachen-grundefur-einen-unruhigen-oder-gestresstenhund?_pos=2&_sid=6cbdeab49&_ss=r

Die verschiedenen Lernformen beim Hund | Animalia. (o. D.). Animalia. Abgerufen am 9. August 2022, von https://www.animalia-sa.ch/de/ratgeber/die-verschiedenen-lernformen-beim-hund

Warum knabbert der Hund an mir? (2022, 9. Februar). Petplan DE. Abgerufen am 23. August 2022, von https://petplan.de/warum-knabbert-der-hund-an-mir/

Wie dem Hund das Bellen abgewöhnen wenn es an der Haustür klingelt. (o. D.). nutricanis. Abgerufen am 13. August 2022, von https://www.nutricanis.de/hund-bellt-an-dertuer/#:%7E:text=Fazit%3A%20Warum%20der%20Hund%20bellt,meist%20auch%20wieder%20abtrainiert%20werde

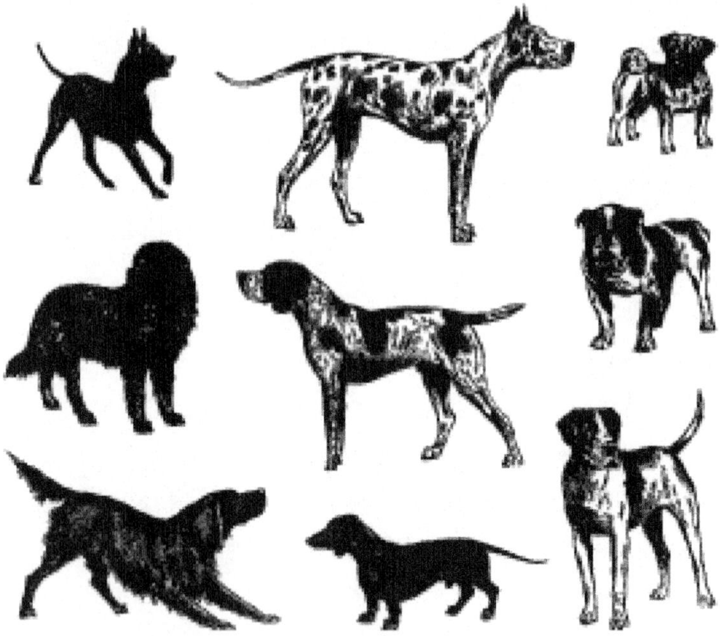

Printed in Great Britain
by Amazon